REALITY CHECK FOR THE CHURCH

Discovering a Unique Vision for the Small Church

*To Andrew
Thanks for attending
the retreat
Phil 3:10
Ron Johnston*

Dr. Ron Johnston

REALITY CHECK FOR THE CHURCH
Copyright © 2013 by Dr. Ron Johnston

All rights reserved. Neither this publication nor any part of this publication may be reproduced or transmitted in any form or by any means, electronic or mechanical, including photocopying, recording or any information storage and retrieval system, without permission in writing from the author.

Scripture taken from the Holy Bible, NEW INTERNATIONAL VERSION®. Copyright © 1973, 1978, 1984 by Biblica, Inc. All rights reserved worldwide. Used by permission. NEW INTERNATIONAL VERSION® and NIV® are registered trademarks of Biblica, Inc. Use of either trademark for the offering of goods or services requires the prior written consent of Biblica US, Inc.

Printed in Canada

ISBN: 978-1-4866-0110-3

Word Alive Press
131 Cordite Road, Winnipeg, MB R3W 1S1
www.wordalivepress.ca

Cataloguing in Publication information may be obtained through Library and Archives Canada

This book is dedicated to
the four people who most closely
walked with me through the
experience of being a pastor.

To my wife, Gloria,
and
our three children,
Darrell, Melanie and Anita

TABLE OF CONTENTS

Acknowledgements	vii
Preface	ix
Introduction	xi

STEP ONE: Clearly Define Your Reality — 1
CHAPTER ONE: THE IMPORTANCE OF A REALITY CHECK — 3
CHAPTER TWO: KEYS TO DISCOVERING REALITY — 19

STEP TWO: Intentionally Grow Your Leadership — 31
CHAPTER THREE: THE KIND OF LEADERS CHURCHES NEED — 33

STEP THREE: Enthusiastically Embrace Your Uniqueness — 51
CHAPTER FOUR: THE UNIQUENESS OF YOUR CHURCH — 53
CHAPTER FIVE: THE UNIQUENESS OF THE SMALL CHURCH — 66

STEP FOUR: Carefully Rethink Your Mission — 87
CHAPTER SIX: THE MISSION OF GOD — 89
CHAPTER SEVEN: THE KINGDOM OF GOD — 96
CHAPTER EIGHT: THE DANGER OF DEFINING CONVERSION TOO NARROWLY — 103

STEP FIVE: Expectantly Shape Your Vision — 111
CHAPTER NINE: THE IMPORTANCE OF VISION — 113

| CHAPTER TEN: BUILDING A VISION | 130 |
| CHAPTER ELEVEN: THE PLACE OF PRAYER | 145 |

Conclusion	148
About the Author	151
Bibliography	152
Footnotes	156

ACKNOWLEDGEMENTS

This book has been written out of a lifetime spent in small church settings. The foundation for my faith and my passion for ministry was formed in childhood and teenage years in the context of two small churches in rural Ontario: the Sundridge Gospel Mission and the Burks Falls Baptist Church. I had the privilege of serving as pastor in small churches for more than twenty years. Today I still attend a small church. In all of those settings numerous people have contributed to both my passion for the small church and my understanding of small-church life. I could not begin to name all of them, but I do thank each and everyone.

Doug Loveday was my thesis supervisor and, as such, helped to shape an important part of this book. Doug, I treasured our times together and have appreciated your friendship over the years. Marilyn Draper, Paul Atkinson, Russ and Jan Martin, Mark McCready, Bevin Mortley and France Young read the full manuscript of either the thesis or this book. Their input contributed greatly to the finished product.

I am the proud father of three children and grandfather of seven grandchildren, for whom I thank God each and every day. My children had to endure the good and the bad that goes with being a pastor's child. They did so without ever complaining. Some of the experiences that shaped my thinking and my life were not easy to go through, but the unfailing love of my children helped to make them bearable.

My wife has walked with me every step of my journey as a pastor, and no one in ministry ever received more support from a spouse than

I did from mine. I am nervous about trying to write this paragraph because I know I could never properly express my appreciation for the blessing that Gloria has been to me. She has shared in the blessings and made them more enjoyable because she was part of them. She has sacrificed more times than I could count. She has supported and encouraged me through all the tough times that ministry involves. We have been married for almost forty-three years, and I am more in love with her than I have ever been. Gloria, thank you for sharing my life and my ministry with me. No one has done more to shape my life and my ministry in a positive way than you.

PREFACE

Last year I successfully defended a thesis that was part of a doctor of ministry program at Acadia Divinity College. The subject of the thesis was *Evangelism in the Small Church.* This book combines the academic research that went into the writing of that thesis with the practical lessons learned from almost forty years of Christian ministry. The reader will probably be able to distinguish between the parts that have come out of the thesis and those parts based largely on personal experience by the number of footnotes at the bottom of the pages.

While it is my hope that people from every size of church will be able to benefit from what I have written, the book is written primarily for leaders in small churches. I believe that the small church has a special place in God's plan. Scores of people have been powerfully impacted by the small churches that they grew up in or that they currently attend. Considering that there are more small churches in the world than all other sizes combined, there are not nearly enough resources being designed to meet the unique issues that these churches face. It is my prayer that this volume will fill some of that void.

In writing about the church there is always a tension between the need to address the practical, hands-on issues on the one hand and the spiritual realities that play a large part in the church's success on the other. This book is designed to address those practical issues, but at the heart of everything needs to be spiritual dynamics such as faith and prayer. I will address these at the end of the book, but I have written from the perspective that the need for prayer and the place of faith are understood.

Each major section in the book has a four-word title to describe it, and each of the words has been carefully selected to complement the other three. Each title ends with a noun that describes the major focus of the section. Thus the book deals with reality, leadership, uniqueness, mission and vision. The third word in each title is the possessive adjective "your." The book doesn't deal with these subjects in abstraction. Rather it is the reality, leadership, uniqueness, mission and vision in each reader's church that the book is addressing. The second word is a verb that describes the specific action that needs to be taken. Thus reality needs to be defined, leadership needs to be grown, uniqueness needs to be embraced, mission needs to be rethought, and vision needs to be shaped. Finally, the first word describes how these actions need to be carried out. The adverb that begins each title may be the most important word. Thus reality must be defined, but it must be defined clearly. Leadership must be grown, but it must be grown intentionally. Uniqueness must be embraced, but it must be embraced enthusiastically. Mission must be rethought, but it must be rethought carefully. Finally, vision must be shaped, but it must be shaped expectantly.

One of the important issues over the past few decades has been the need for language that reflects the important role women have played in the life of the church. Throughout the book I have tried to intersperse feminine and masculine pronouns to reflect the fact that both men and women are being used by God to impact the world around us. Both men and women are increasingly taking positions of leadership in our churches, and language should reflect that fact. Whatever position a person might take on the gender issue in the church, no one can deny that both sexes have been used by God to carry out his mission in the world.

This book is addressed to anyone who loves the church. Jesus told his disciples that he would build his church (Matthew 16:18), and that building process is still being carried out today and will be until Jesus returns in triumph and brings history as we know it to a close.

INTRODUCTION

For the past twenty years or so I have lived with a personal commitment to a value that has helped to shape my life. It gives every day that I live purpose. It is what makes it worth getting out of bed in the morning. It turns every day into an adventure.

Here it is:

Every day I want my life to touch the life of at least one other person in such a way that the other person is brought into a closer relationship with Jesus Christ.

It doesn't have to be in a big way. I don't have to be the person who brings radical life-changing transformation that turns people into spiritual giants. I just want to make a difference in someone's walk with God. I want someone's life to be richer because I was a small part of it.

As I look back over the years, I wish I had developed that value long before I did. It would have saved me considerable pain and frustration. I preached my first sermon when I was a teenager. Before long I was being asked to speak in a variety of settings and was receiving some very nice compliments after I preached. I remember one person in particular who compared me to Billy Graham and who predicted great things for me in the future. I began to think that just maybe those people were right. Maybe I was destined for greatness.

It took me a long time to learn that when you're a teenage preacher, people are just thrilled about the fact that you're a teenager and you're preaching. You don't need particularly good content. You don't have to have very much skill as a communicator. The main thing that you have going for you is that you are young. Many people, and especially those in their senior years, love to see younger people involved in ministry.

It took me a long time to understand that greatness has very little to do with our accomplishments. It has everything to do with our character. It has very little to do with numbers. It has everything to do with changed lives. As I look back now, I realize that some of the greatest people I have ever known spent their whole lives in obscurity but touched lives one person at a time.

I share all of this to say that I am no one special. I have never pastored a large church. I have never preached to the multitudes and had throngs of people respond to my message. I have never had to hire anyone to handle my schedule because I couldn't keep up with the invitations coming my way from every corner of the world. I am just an ordinary person who has made more than my share of mistakes.

So what gives me the audacity to write still another book about churches? I am always a little nervous about listing my credentials because I know that an author can make them say anything he wishes. I've spent a lot of my life in school and have acquired a few degrees along the way. I have spent almost four decades in full-time Christian ministry. I have been able to visit churches around the world and have taught on four different continents. I have never been impressed with anyone's credentials, least of all my own, and so I won't bore you with the details.

I think two things give me some credibility as an author on this subject. The first is that I love the local church. I've spent most of my life serving in a local church. I've seen the church in all its glory, and I have suffered with it when it has failed. I've experienced the love and support that only the church can give, and I've been deeply hurt by the very people I served. I have no illusions about the church being perfect or even close to perfect, but I love it just the same.

Every so often I return to Ray Stedman's description of the church that I first read back in the seventies. After outlining a host of ways in which the church has failed over the years he says this:

INTRODUCTION

Let us be perfectly honest and admit that the church has often been all these things, at many times and places. It has amply justified every bitter charge leveled against it. Nevertheless, despite its many weaknesses and its tragic sins the church has been, in every century since its inception, the most powerful force for good on the face of the earth. It has been light in the midst of darkness so dense it could be felt. It has been salt in society, retarding the spread of moral corruption and adding zest and flavor to human life.[1]

I get goose bumps whenever I read that description because that is what I want to be part of. I believe in the local church, with all of its failures. This is not a book written by an outside critic but by someone on the inside who is passionately in love with and deeply committed to the church.

The second qualification is that I have made my share of mistakes. Almost every book on leadership that I've read has made the point that a leader isn't the person who has never failed but rather the person who is able to get up, dust himself off and keep trying. If that is true, then I have met at least one of the criteria for a good leader. I have made more than my share of mistakes.

Why is making mistakes a credential for writing this book? For the most part I have learned from my mistakes, and it is those lessons that I will be sharing in this book. Without the mistakes, I wouldn't have anything to write.

A few years ago I had the opportunity to serve as the interim pastor in a wonderful church in Alliston, Ontario. One of the leaders in that church said some nice things about me and the leadership I had provided. I reminded him that whatever skills I had demonstrated in that setting had been developed on the back of a host of mistakes that I had made in other churches. That is true for any pastor. Lessons aren't learned out of perfection. They are learned in the school of mistakes.

With that in mind, I am going to share some of my life with you in the pages that follow. I am not going to say very much about the successes that I have had, because while I enjoyed them, I didn't learn very much from them. It was the failures that proved to be the most powerful teachers. It is my prayer that in reading this book some of you will be able to learn from my mistakes so that, in at least some areas of church life, you won't have to go through the pain of making your own.

This book is designed to help small churches develop a vision that is uniquely theirs, both as small churches and as individual churches that are different from every other church on earth. There are five steps that touch on five important elements of church life. In the first section, churches are called upon to clearly define their own reality and in so doing discover exactly who they are. The second section encourages the church to intentionally grow its leadership, because strong leadership is essential to a healthy church. The third section helps the church enthusiastically embrace its uniqueness. Your church is different from all other churches, and it is important to discover those qualities that are uniquely yours. The small church is also different from the medium-sized or large church and certainly different from the mega-church. The fourth section looks at some theological issues that will help the church to carefully rethink its mission. Finally, the fifth section will help the church expectantly shape its vision. While it may be tempting to jump to the final chapter in order to see what that vision might look like, I encourage you to resist the temptation. The final chapter is built on the principles shared in the earlier ones.

I mentioned at the beginning that my personal goal is to touch at least one person each day in a way that brings that person into closer relationship with Jesus Christ. My prayer for this book is that the Holy Spirit will use it to bring whole churches into a deeper, more vital relationship with Christ. I don't necessarily wish numerical growth for your church, although those growth periods can be exciting, challenging times. What I do wish is that your church will come to see Jesus Christ at work in people's lives in such a way that they get a renewed faith in his power and presence, not only in the church but in each of their lives as well. If numerical growth comes along with that renewed life, that will be an added bonus.

STEP ONE
Clearly Define Your Reality

ONE

The Importance of a Reality Check

Four months before I graduated from Bible college, I entered into my first pastorate. Like many grads fresh from the academic wars, I envisioned accomplishing great things for God and establishing my own reputation at the same time. I knew that this was no ordinary church to which I had been called. This was a church with a future, and I was going to be the leader who led them into that future.

In my last year of study I was introduced to the church growth movement with its origins in Fuller Seminary. If you know anything about this movement, you know it did not encourage small thinking. From reading, in particular the books of C. Peter Wagner, I discovered that God wanted my church to grow, and if it didn't grow, something was seriously wrong. Wagner made it clear that just as growth is a natural part of the physical realm, so it is in the spiritual realm as well. The basic message of this movement was that healthy churches grow.

> God's will is clear. He does not desire that "any should perish but that all should come to repentance" (2 Peter 3:9). He wants men and women everywhere to come to Him and into the church of Jesus Christ. In short, it is God's will that churches grow.[2]

During those early years in my first church, I read everything that I could get my hands on related to church growth. I believed that growth was part of God's plan for every church, and, naturally, that included my small church.

That first church numbered a little over one hundred in Sunday morning attendance. It had been that size for a long time, but I was confident that there were greater days ahead. All I had to do was have faith and follow the guidelines laid out for me in the books I was reading. Spectacular growth was just around the corner.

At some point in that first year, I made the audacious announcement that there was no reason we could not become a church of more than one thousand people. I'm not sure why I didn't go even larger in my dreams, but one thousand seemed like a nice round number. After all, we were an urban church with limitless possibilities. The key was to dream big and to trust God to bring our dreams to fulfillment. I had read that I had to not only believe in my goals but share them as well. So I made the announcement. I told the congregation we were on our way to becoming one of the largest churches in the city.

Three years later I was fired. The church was smaller than it was when I started. A number of key families had moved to a new, much larger church down the street. We were in decline, and there didn't seem to be anything I could do to turn things around.

One of the unalterable laws of professional sport is that if a team is performing poorly, the owner can't fire the entire team. So, he fires the coach. One of the laws of church life is that if a church is performing poorly, they can't fire the entire congregation. So, they fire the pastor. That is what happened in my case. Actually, to be precise, I wasn't fired, but it was made clear to me that, whether I resigned or was fired, my days at that church were numbered. I took the route I believed would be less harmful to the church and handed in my resignation.

So what went wrong? What happened to those marvelous dreams that had seemed so real, so possible, just a few short years before? There were many reasons for our perceived failure, but one stands out. It was true of me as the pastor, and it was true of the congregation as well.

None of us were willing to face reality.

As I look back from the perspective of time and a great deal more experience, I realize that there was very little possibility that the church would grow. There were at least three major obstacles in the way, and we weren't prepared to face any of them.

First, the church was not prepared to make the changes required for it to grow. "The indispensable condition for a growing church is that it wants to grow and is willing to pay the price for that growth."[3] In that one sentence Wagner defined the problem for the people in that first church. Growth would have involved change, and they were not about to make the changes required. There was a price tag, and the people were definitely not willing to pay the price. They had become comfortable in their smallness, and while they would have said that they wanted growth, they didn't want it enough to change.

The second limitation lay in the fact that our location was terrible. We were nestled back into a residential neighbourhood, which limited our growth potential. We were located on the edge of the fastest growing Jewish community in the city, which seriously limited the possibility for any significant growth coming from the area right around the church building. Furthermore, we were a church designed to attract young couples, but the cost of housing meant that few young couples were able to afford to live close enough to make us their church home. All of these factors added up to a very limited potential for growth.

The last limitation is the most difficult to admit, but admit it I must. Time and experience have brought me to the place where I am willing to acknowledge a difficult truth. I am not Rick Warren or Bill Hybels or any of the other pastors whose names were on everyone's tongue when I was trying to grow this church. I do not have that special gift-mix that enables a person to take a church with a few hundred in membership and turn it into a mega-church with membership in the thousands. I know that often in church growth seminars you are told that anyone can grow a church if they just take the proper steps, but that simply isn't true. The reason that there are so few mega-churches is that there are very few people with the ability to pastor a church that size.

Someone may be tempted to put on his super-spiritual hat and make the point that it is God who grows a church, and therefore growth isn't dependent on the gift-mix of a pastor. I agree that God gives the growth, but I also know that God uses people. He tends to use highly gifted people in special ways, but there are not very many highly gifted people around. I definitely was not one of those highly gifted people, and, judging by the scarcity of mega-churches in Canada, there aren't many of those kind of people around.

That was the reality that we simply didn't want to face. The church didn't want to admit its unwillingness to grow. We didn't want to look at the demographics that limited our growth potential. I didn't want to face my own limitations and admit that I was best suited to pastor a small church. As a result, growth did not occur, people left the church, and I was fired.

Facing Reality

If we were the only church that failed to face reality, my story wouldn't really matter much. But we are not. In fact, almost every church with which I have had any association has failed at this point. Churches will try new programs, hire new staff, implement a new vision and make a multitude of other changes, but they will not look the truth about themselves full in the face and honestly embrace reality.

I believe that failure to face reality is the number one obstacle to effectiveness in most churches, and when churches aren't effective, bad things happen. Stagnation sets in. People migrate to other churches. Pastors get fired. Churches give up hope. Most serious of all, God's Kingdom suffers.

This book is all about facing reality in our churches. This is never an easy thing to do, but it is an indispensable step in planning for the future.

In his excellent book *Integrity*, Dr. Henry Cloud put it well:

> One of my favorite sayings is, no matter how difficult it is to hear, reality is always your friend. The reason is almost a truism: everything else is a fantasy. So, for us to get real results in the real world, *we must be in touch with what is, not what we wish things were or think things should be or are led by others to believe they are. The only thing that is going to be real in the end is what is.*[4]

Like millions of other people, in the early years of the new millennium I became completely engrossed in the wonderful fantasy world portrayed in the Lord of the Rings movie trilogy. I could hardly wait for each new installment to be released so that I could once again lose myself in the world of hobbits, wizards and magic rings. I was in awe of Tolkien's ability to create this wonderful new world and of Peter Jackson's ability to bring it to the screen. As brilliant as their work was, I knew that the world of Middle Earth was fantasy, the product of someone's imagination. Whenever we fail to face reality, we are living in our own Middle Earth. A fantasy world is a wonderful place in which to escape but a dangerous place in which to live. That is just as true for churches as it is for individuals.

Anyone who has undertaken major renovations on his house knows that they always take longer, cost more and are messier than expected. That is a good description for what can happen in our churches when we search for reality. Distinguishing between the fantasy world in which many churches live and reality can take longer, cost more and be messier than we ever dreamed, but in the end it is worth the effort.

Reality Distorters

Why is reality so difficult to discover? Mainly because there are a number of things that tend to distort our view. For several years I lived in the town of Parkhill in southwestern Ontario. One of the benefits was that I got to enjoy some of the most beautiful sunsets in the world. The land is flat, and there is nothing to obscure the view when the sun goes down. I grew up in the Parry Sound district in the heart of Ontario's cottage country, an area filled with hills, lakes and bush. The beauty of the sunset might have been almost comparable to southwestern Ontario, but I could never really see one, because of the hills and the trees. Without an unobstructed view I couldn't tell what a sunset really looked like there.

Reality involves getting an accurate view of our church, free of all the things that tend to distort and obscure our perspective. We need to somehow clear the hills and the bush away so that we can see what the sunset really looks like. We need to discover reality, with all that that entails. We need to see our churches as they really are.

What are the things that obscure our view? As is true of most lists, the following is not all-inclusive, but it does contain some of the more serious distorters.

Fear of Hurting People

David Hansen talks about the temptation we all face of building a dream church in our minds rather than dealing with the actual church of which we are a part. The dream church is made up of perfect people who love each other and never make mistakes. But as Hansen points out, that is not reality.

> Jesus dwells in the church that actually exists, not in the ideal church that exists in my mind. The actual church is made up of sinful people and served by a sinful pastor. The actual church is where Jesus lives, the church that Jesus is building, the church that Jesus died for. We have no reason to believe that Jesus cares about our ideal church at all.[5]

In the real church, made up of redeemed sinners, reality is often the last thing that we are looking for. We don't want to be told that our program doesn't fit into the overall vision of the church. We don't want to be told that our reaction to something was not appropriate. We don't want to be told that as a church we are failing in some vital aspect of church life. Sometimes people can only grow into spiritual maturity by being hurt, but it doesn't make it any easier when we are the ones who have to do the hurting.

Most churches take the easy way out and never confront people with anything that might cause hurt. The problem is that ultimately non-confrontation does not contribute to the growth of the people involved. As anyone who has ever raised children knows, there are times when, for the good of the person involved, we need to look past the immediate hurt and do whatever is needed for that person's ultimate good.

I spoke in a church a few years ago and experienced firsthand what happens when we allow our fear of hurting people to obscure reality. In this church one man led the singing. The problem was that he was almost deaf and could not hear the piano or the congregation. He was simply singing to his own timing, oblivious to what everyone else in the church was doing. As a result he finished every verse of every hymn at least four or five beats after everyone else was finished. This man had been a respected leader in that church for a long time. He had been an excellent song leader over the years, but those years were in the past. If it hadn't been so sad, it would have been humorous. Reality was that someone who had been a respected leader in that local church and in the larger evangelical world was now laughed at as he tried to lead the singing and failed. There were children who only knew him as the deaf man who still tried to lead singing every Sunday. His reputation was damaged because no one had the courage to talk with him and make him face reality.

In their book *Boundaries in Marriage*, Dr. Henry Cloud and Dr. John Townsend point out that "just because someone is in pain doesn't necessarily mean something bad is happening."[6] Pain can be a necessary part of growth. When we avoid reality rather than confront someone, in far too many cases we are robbing people of the opportunity to grow. As will be pointed out in more detail later in the book, growth into discipleship should be the primary objective of every church. Such growth cannot happen in people's lives unless we allow them to experience pain.

James, the brother of Jesus, understood this principle when he wrote to Jewish believers in the first century,

> *Consider it pure joy, my brothers, whenever you face trials of many kinds, because you know that the testing of your faith develops perseverance. Perseverance must finish its work so that you may be mature and complete, not lacking anything.* (James 1:2–4)

It is important to note that James is not saying that we need to give thanks for trials. Trials are never easy. In the case of some trials there is a great deal of pain and suffering that people have to endure, and pain hurts. One of the lessons I learned in my years as a pastor is that we need to be very careful to not give trite answers to people who are going through trials, because the pain that they are feeling is very real.

There is, however, another side to the equation. While pain is never easy to go through, there is growth that can only occur in the midst of pain. It is that growth for which we need to be thankful. It is when our faith is tested that we develop perseverance, and it is perseverance that ultimately brings us to maturity. When we try to shield people from having to experience any pain in their lives, we rob them of the chance to grow. We prevent them from ever reaching maturity in their walk with the Lord, and *that* must be the ultimate goal for every Christian.

Fear of Change

Is there any word more dreaded in our churches than *change*? Most people at the very least shy away from it, while some people do almost anything to avoid it completely. There is something comforting about the status quo. Someone defined *status quo* as being Latin for the mess we're in, but for a lot of people the mess we're in is better than the uncertainty of the mess we might create if we change things.

A few years ago I accepted an invitation from a small church to meet with some of the leadership and attend one of their meetings. I enjoyed a delicious supper at the home of one of the key leaders and then drove with him to the meeting. On the way there he tried to prepare me for the evening ahead. He said they were a very progressive congregation that had moved a long way from the traditions of their denominational background.

Just a short time into the meeting that night, I realized that I was in one of the most traditional churches that I had visited in quite some time. They could have been used as the poster church for everything that had characterized churches of that tradition for the past hundred years. Almost nothing of any significance had changed from the way that their parents would have done things. Since almost every church that I visit tells me that they lie on the more progressive side of the continuum, I added this one to the list of those that did not have an accurate view of themselves when it came to change.

Facing reality almost always brings us face to face with the need for change. As long as we live in a fantasy world of our own creation, we can pretend that we are progressive or contemporary or whatever other word we might want to use, and we can feel good about ourselves. When we really face the truth about ourselves, it becomes much more difficult to live with the status quo. Often, reality demands change.

A few years ago, a pastor told me about a conversation that he had with a person who had grown up in his church. She was married and had been away from the church for a number of years. She told the pastor that there was one thing she really enjoyed about returning to that church. She knew that nothing ever changed. Everything was just like it had been when she was a child, and as a result, she experienced a sense of well-being whenever she returned.

After thinking about this conversation for a while, the pastor decided it wasn't the kind of compliment he really wanted to receive. He didn't want to hear that even though people had been away from the church for a decade or more, they could feel right at home because nothing had changed in their absence. That was a reality that he didn't want to face and certainly didn't want to live with.

The reality is that even in churches where people may not notice change, change is constantly happening. There is no such thing in any church as the status quo. People get older. Young people grow up and move out of the area. Babies are born. Church members, sometimes even those who have been members for a long time, leave the church for a variety of reasons. New people move into the community and begin to attend. People resign from positions of leadership, and new leaders take their place. In one church in which I served as pastor, they went from having a solid Sunday school program and a very small youth group to having a struggling Sunday school and a youth group that was bursting at the seams. The change happened over the course of a few years simply because the children who had made up the Sunday school became teenagers. The families who had had young children when I first went there had high-schoolers five years later.

Change will happen, and there's nothing any church can do to stop it. The key question is, what will the church do to manage that change?

Most churches are reactive in their response to change. Change occurs, and then they react to it. Successful churches are proactive in their management of change. They plan for change before it ever takes place. The key to being proactive is a clear understanding of reality.

Fear of Theological Uncertainty

As I was writing this section, I received an email from Tyndale University College and Seminary. I graduated from both the college and seminary, and the email said that one of the teachers I had at both levels had recently died. Dr. Don Leggett taught for more than forty years, and I had the privilege of taking several courses with him. As valuable as those classes were, a statement he made outside of the formal teaching time made the greatest impact on my life. He said if a person isn't living with tension in his understanding of Scripture, he isn't understanding the Bible correctly. As I applied that to my own life, I came to understand that if my interpretation of Scripture fit neatly into my theological package without any loose ends sticking out, my theological system was my authority rather than Scripture. Part of Dr. Leggett's legacy for me has been that over the years the areas of certainty in my theological understanding have grown fewer and the areas of tension have increased. It is a more difficult place in which to live but one that more accurately reflects the truth of Scripture.

I grew up in a church setting in which certainty was held up as an ideal. We were dispensational in our theology, Baptist in our ecclesiology and fundamentalist in our approach to Christian living. There were only two groups of people—those who were wrong, and us. We had a monopoly on the truth, which meant that anyone who disagreed with us had to be in the group that was wrong. With that background, you can understand why I found Dr. Leggett's words life-changing.

A lot of people do not want to live with tension in their theology. They enjoy having a nice neat system into which every verse of Scripture and every part of life can be made to fit. Reality has a way of forcing us to re-examine our theological and ecclesiological systems. A lot of people don't want to do that.

Over the past quarter century, churches, academic institutions, parachurch organizations and individuals have tried to come to terms with the gender issue in Christian ministry. In an attempt to understand the questions surrounding this issue, I have read books, taken a seminary course, listened to debates and spent countless hours in personal study. As a result, I have come to appreciate how many different views there are on the subject. My personal position on the issue has certainly changed, but I have also come to appreciate that this is one of those areas of tension about which Dr. Leggett warned me. There isn't a simple answer that neatly takes care of all the loose ends. An honest evaluation of the biblical evidence necessitates that we live with some theological tension.

The problem, though, is that our culture has radically changed. Women, today, are difference makers at every level of society. They hold cabinet posts in our national government. They fill CEO positions in highly successful multi-national corporations. They make major contributions to the arts, sciences, sports and every other field of endeavour that shapes our lives in the twenty-first century. In the broader culture it is no longer acceptable to question the value of the contribution to our society that women make.

As churches continue to examine the practical implications of this, they need to look not only at the theological and biblical issues involved but also at the reality of the role that the women in their congregation play in the wider society outside of the church. This may lead to some theological tension, but they need to be willing to live with that tension in the decisions they make. This is but one example of the kind of issues with which churches need to deal today.

The first-century church knew what it was to live with theological tension. Whether the people in a church were from a Jewish background, such as in the church in Jerusalem, or from a Greek background, such as in most of the churches that Paul planted, their theological foundations would have been shaken to the very core of their being. For those with a Jewish background, the truth that Jesus was God would have been earth-shattering. They had been raised with the reality that there was one God, and that truth set them apart from every other religion in the world around them. They were the only monotheistic religion in the world of their day, and they were proud of that fact. It was what made their belief system different from all of the false religions. Then they had to come to terms with the fact that this Jewish man who lived among them and died on the cross for their sins was God. While today we understand this in light of a fully developed theology of the Trinity, for a person coming out of a first-century Jewish backiground, this had to be a huge tension.

On the other hand, Greek believers had been raised with just the opposite belief. There was a god for every occasion. In Athens there was even an altar to the "unknown god." Now they had to adjust their thinking to the fact that there is only one God and this Jewish Messiah is that God. One God created the world. One God sovereignly oversees the affairs of humankind. All of these multiple gods that they had worshipped all of their lives were just worthless idols with no real power to influence their future. That was the tension for Greek believers.

Whether it was first century Christians wrestling with the deity of Jesus Christ or it is twenty-first century Christians wrestling with the gender issue, theological tension is a part of what it means to be a follower of Jesus Christ. The only way to avoid that kind of tension is by allowing our neatly packaged theological systems to shape our beliefs rather than coming to Scripture with an open mind and allowing the Word of God with all of its tensions to do that shaping for us.

Fear of Failure

The year 1941 was a baseball season to remember. Two things happened that year that have not happened since and may never happen again. Joe DiMaggio of the New York Yankees hit safely in fifty-six consecutive games, setting a record that has become one of the most revered in baseball. Not to be outdone, Ted Williams of the rival Boston Red Sox hit .406, and no one has hit for a higher average in the more than seventy years that have passed since he accomplished that feat. Williams may be the best hitter ever to have played the game, and yet in what may have been his greatest year, he only hit .400. That means that in six out of every ten at bats he failed. He didn't succeed even 50 percent of the time.

Failure is a part of every life, but we don't like to face it. Much of the time we live in a fantasy world in which we pretend that failure doesn't really exist. If this is true in our individual lives, it is also true in our corporate lives as churches. Too often we imitate the ostrich by burying our heads in the sand, hoping that our failures will just go away.

When I was in my twenties, I had the opportunity to be part of the leadership of an outreach team in Toronto for two weeks. About fifty young people came from all over Canada and the United States to try to reach people with the gospel in this great cosmopolitan city. Mostly they went door-to-door with surveys designed to lead into opportunities to share their faith. They also did street evangelism and helped with some local church programs. It was an amazing two weeks as these young people shared their faith and tried to introduce people to Jesus Christ. The highlight of every day was the sharing time in the evening when people would tell about the chances to witness that they had had that day. Every night there were stories about how people had come to faith in Christ. I still look back on that experience as one of the wonderful opportunities that God gave me to be involved in an exciting ministry.

About a year after the team had disbanded and returned to the far corners of the continent, I spoke with the key leader who had organized the whole project. We were talking about the great time that we had had with all those young adults when I asked the question that I probably wasn't supposed to ask. I asked him if he knew of anyone brought to faith through the work of the team who was involved in a church and was growing in his or her walk with God. His answer was one of the things that caused me to take a second look at much of what we called evangelism in our churches. He did not know of even one person who would fit the three criteria that I had outlined. There wasn't one person who a year later was involved in a church and growing in faith. That was reality, and it caused me to look at something that I had seen as a highly successful experience and instead admit that, while it wasn't a total failure, it certainly wasn't the success that I had thought it was. No program that provides an avenue for fifty young people to share their faith could be described as a total failure, but as an outreach event it certainly had not achieved the goals that had been set for it. That was not an easy pill to swallow. Failure never is.

Fear of failure can paralyze people so that they don't even try to reach beyond their present situation and achieve their goals. I am writing this section on New Year's Day, and like so many other people I have already made a bunch of resolutions for the year ahead. Like so many other people, I have resolved to lose weight this year. This isn't a new resolution. Rather it is one that I have set for myself every year for a number of years, and every year I have failed to lose the weight that I hoped to lose. There are few areas in which I have failed more consistently than this one. If I just don't set any weight-loss goals for this year, I won't have to worry about failure. I won't lose any weight, but at least I won't fail to live up to my resolution. I have determined though that I'm not going to allow a fear of failure to keep me from changing my lifestyle. One of my goals for this year is to shed the pounds that I need to shed.

There is a less obvious but just as deadly response to a fear of failure, and it often characterizes churches. Rather than allowing a fear of failure to paralyze them, some people simply ignore reality and in so doing never admit their failure. They still set their goals to lose weight, but they never step on the scales to see if they are losing the weight or not. Churches that fall into this category may begin programs or set goals, but they don't have any measurements that they then apply to those programs or goals to determine if they are succeeding or not. They never evaluate anything that they do to determine its impact. They never face reality, because reality has a way of forcing us to confront our failures face to face.

Fear of Not Getting My Own Way

While attending a conference a few years ago, I realized that the group leading worship in the evening session employed a worship style that I strongly disliked. Instead of looking forward to the evening as I had every other session in the conference, I found myself dreading it. I just knew that this was not going to be an enjoyable experience.

The group lived up to all of my worst expectations. From the very first song I knew that this was going to be a long evening. Then God impressed an important truth on my mind. I couldn't do anything about the worship style or the group that was leading, but I could do something about my reaction. I could sit there with a bad attitude, feeling sorry for myself and critical of everything that was happening on the platform, or I could change my attitude and participate in a time of worship. I didn't have to think very hard to decide which of those two options was more honouring to God.

I knew that in my own power I wasn't going to change, so I prayed a very short but powerful prayer. I asked God to do what I couldn't do. I asked Him to change my attitude so that I could enter fully into the time of corporate worship. He did, and I enjoyed a very meaningful worship time. What is so amazing about God's grace is that He pours it into our lives when we deserve it least, and for me this was one of those times.

At the heart of my response was the realization that worship style is largely a matter of personal preference. There were scores of other people at that conference who loved the worship band. My reaction was not based on any theological truth but simply on my own personal preference. I still don't like that particular style, but so what? It's just my preference.

In identifying reality in our churches we need to make sure that we don't get caught up in areas of personal preference. As we try to define reality, we need to make a clear distinction between areas that are matters of subjective choice and areas that are objective fact. I've mentioned worship style, but I could have referred to many other aspects of church life. We all have preferences, and there is nothing wrong with that. The danger comes when we insist that those preferences are biblical and hence the only way to do things.

One of the most important conferences ever held in the history of the church is recorded in the fifteenth chapter of the book of Acts. The leadership in the church met to decide whether being a Christian was going to be defined by Jewish standards or whether God was doing something entirely new that was going to require a new understanding of how God works. Christians from a Jewish background were saying that a Christian still had to follow Jewish traditions. Those leaders who had been working with Gentile believers stated that the gospel was revolutionary and that they needed a new understanding of what God was doing. The first group said that circumcision was still a necessary part of a man's relationship with God. The second group saw this as insisting that an adherence to the law was essential to salvation, and they asserted that salvation was on the basis of faith alone. The leaders heard both sides and then handed down their decision, that it was wrong to insist that Gentiles be circumcised. God was indeed doing something entirely new, and the Jewish believers shouldn't insist that their preference for the Jewish law needed to be applied to everyone. If the Jewish Christians had insisted on their own preferences, the early church would have been split into Jewish and Gentile sects, with all of the damage that would have come from such a split in the early decades of Christianity.

Summary

One of the most important lessons that I have learned is that often there is more than one reaction that people have to change. There is an intellectual assent to change that often happens at a business meeting when the change is discussed and the vote to make a change is taken. At that time people are impressed with the logic of the move and are willing to vote that the church should move in the new direction. There is often a very different reaction when the change is actually put into place and the implications of the change are experienced. Then people respond with their emotions. The very person who voted in the affirmative is suddenly strongly opposed to the change, and the leadership is left wondering what happened. What happened is that people weren't given the time to make the emotional adjustments needed for them to be totally in favour of the change.

When the importance of reality has been acknowledged and the obstacles to discovering reality have been noted, the next step is to determine what reality truly is. At this point a church needs to proceed with caution. People may have given an intellectual assent to discovering reality, but they also need to be given time to make the emotional adjustments. The next chapter provides some guidelines for making this discovery and some steps that can minimize the emotional impact.

TWO

Keys to Discovering Reality

How does a church discover reality? If the people within a church do not want to face reality, they will never find it. The steps that follow are designed to help you identify the truth about your church, but the people within your church must have a desire to discover it.

When I was a student in Bible college, I heard about a Christian organization that broadcast a radio program for children every Saturday morning. In trying to determine their effectiveness they hired an outside consultant to find out exactly who was listening to their program. The consultant determined that the average listener to their children's program was a woman in her seventies. Their response to this was to ignore the findings of the consultant and continue broadcasting without making any changes. I don't know if that story is true, but it illustrates one of the problems in our churches. Even when we discover reality, there can be a tendency to ignore it and continue on doing exactly what we did before.

Solomon, the wisest man who ever lived, described the process we need to go through if we are to find wisdom:

> *My son, if you accept my words and store up my commands within you, turning your ear to wisdom and applying your heart to understanding, and if you call out for insight and cry aloud for understanding, and if you look for it as for silver and search for it as for hidden treasure, then you will understand the fear of the LORD and find the knowledge of God.* (Proverbs 2:1–5)

I've always been impressed with Solomon's description here. Finding wisdom is tough. It takes blood, sweat and tears. You really have to want it. You don't get wisdom unless you put everything you have into the search. But at the end of the search, *"you will understand the fear of the LORD and find the knowledge of God."* It doesn't come easy, but it is always worth the search.

The same is true of reality. The search can be difficult. It may lead in directions that you don't really want to go. It may force you to make decisions that you would sooner not make. But at the end of the search you will understand God's plan for your church. A clear understanding of reality is always worth the search.

The following guidelines are designed to help you discover reality in your church. There is no simple one-two-three-step program that will work in every church, but these steps will take you a long way down the reality path.

1. ASK QUESTIONS

Humility is an indispensable ingredient in defining reality. Humility begins with questions rather than answers. Too often we want instant solutions to all of our problems in our churches, and we don't take the time to clearly define the issues. Before we can define reality we need to gather as much information as possible, and that only comes when we ask questions.

A few years ago I was acting as an advisor for a leadership team in a church. Someone came to the team with a request to start a Friday evening program for children. With a minimum of discussion, permission was given to start the program. This might have been an excellent way for this church to invest its resources, but no questions were ever asked in order to find out if it was.

When we think of resources, often we think only of the financial cost, but that is only the beginning of the cost of running any program. Each person in a church has only a certain number of volunteer hours that he or she can give, which means that when they invest those hours into one program they can't invest them elsewhere. Each program requires someone with leadership skills, and again, those leadership skills can't be invested elsewhere. A program may use the building, which means that other programs can't be run in the building on that night. When calculating costs, we need to take all of these things into consideration.

How many children in the church would attend the program? How many children in the surrounding community might attend the program? Can the program be used as an outreach into the community? How many people will be required to staff the program? Has anything like this been tried before, and if it has, how well did it work? How does the proposed program fit into the overall vision of the church? These and a host of other questions should have been asked before permission was given to start the program.

We need to ask questions not only of new programs but of every aspect of church life. The following five areas of church life are important but certainly not the only areas that need to be included in a search for reality. They will, however, provide the church with a good start on the journey.

The search for reality needs to begin with a clear understanding of **church demographics**. What is the makeup of your church? What is the average attendance on Sunday morning? Most churches tend to exaggerate their attendance figures. An accurate count should be taken over a period of time in order to determine attendance numbers.

What is the makeup of those who attend? What percentage of the congregation consists of seniors, of families, of teenagers, of children? What is the educational level of those who attend on a Sunday morning? How far do people drive in order to be there? How long have people been attending? How many are new to the church in the past year, two years?

A realistic understanding of church demographics should be balanced out by an understanding of **community demographics**. Is the church located in an urban, suburban, small town or rural setting? A church located in the heart of a major city faces a very different situation than a church in a rural setting. What is the ethnic makeup of the community surrounding the church? Does the community consist largely of long-time settled residents or people new to the area? How has the community changed over the past five years, ten years, twenty years?

Do the people who currently attend live in the community in which the church is located? How far do those who live elsewhere have to drive to get to the church?

Once a church has a realistic understanding of both church and community demographics, they need to understand what I am calling their *planning base*. There has been a tendency over the past several decades to introduce business principles into the church. Lyle Schaller notes this tendency and suggests the danger that is involved when a church employs such methods:

> These comments reflect the growing tendency to introduce business methods into the church, to evaluate the worshipping congregation from the perspective of a profit-making corporation and to manage religious organizations in a "businesslike" style. There is a grave risk that an *excessive* emphasis on utilizing business methods in the worshipping congregation can subvert the distinctive nature of the Christian church. There are deep and significant differences between a church and a business. When these differences are overlooked, it is tempting to become more businesslike—and that opens the door to subversion of purpose.[7]

As Schaller points out, there's a fine line between benefiting from the leadership skills that business can provide and allowing those skills to subvert the purpose of the church. A church is not a business, and it needs to have different values and goals from those that a business would have. Profit is not the bottom line. The church has been called to serve God and people, and that should result in decisions that make no sense from a business point of view. Yet there is much that church leaders can learn from books that have been written from a secular perspective.

With this background, what is the planning base for your church? What is the bottom line when making decisions—a balanced budget or human need? What place do values have in the decisions that are made? Are leaders chosen on the basis of their business skills or on the basis of character and spiritual maturity? What is the balance that the church strives to maintain between excellence and relationships?

Earlier I shared the story of the church leader who had a totally unrealistic view of where his church stood on the traditional/progressive continuum. Almost every church would like to think that they are progressive in the way that they do things. They would like to think that they are not controlled by the status quo. It's important to define reality in this regard. Churches that are convinced that the way they do things is the biblical way and nothing should ever change are at one end of the continuum. At the other end are those churches in which almost every decision is determined by the latest trends in society and they are constantly changing. The vast majority of churches don't fall at either extreme.

In determining where a church falls on the continuum, their absolutes must be defined. These are the things that they will not change. A church's statement of faith should fall into this category. They might change the wording, but the basic truths contained in the statement should be set in stone. The message of the gospel that they proclaim should also be absolute. The truths that Jesus Christ died on the cross for our sin and that salvation is on the basis of faith in Christ alone should be non-debatable. On the other hand, the way in which we proclaim those truths needs to be adaptable to the culture around us. Every church is faced with the challenge of determining what is and what is not adaptable.

Finally, churches need to look at reality in regard to their **evangelistic efforts**. Many evangelical churches use outreach to children as an excuse for not reaching out to adults. They run children's clubs throughout the year and day camps in the summer because it is relatively easy to work with children. When asked about their evangelistic efforts, they tell about their various children's programs. I'm all for children's programs. They need to be an important part of our churches, but most churches are doing almost nothing to reach out to adults. Reality is that if we can reach the parents, we will get the children. If we don't get the parents, most of the children will attend our programs when they are young and then disappear, never to be seen in our church or any other church again.

How many adults have been reached through your church over the past two or three years? How many of those adults are attending and serving within your church today? How many of the members within your church are involved in sharing their faith with unchurched people? How much of the church budget is directed towards reaching out to people in the community? How many people within the church are involved in any sort of community activity? How many entry points are there in your church through which people in the community might be able to become involved?

2. LISTEN TO YOUR CRITICS

Criticism is never easy to take, but if we learn to face it properly it can become one of our greatest allies. If our goal is to discover reality, criticism can be one of the primary means by which we do this.

> A very wise man once told me that tucked deep inside every critic's attack is usually at least a tiny kernel of truth. And rather than lashing back, he advised, I should spend my energy figuring out what it is.[8]

When I was a seminary student I took a preaching course. As part of that course I had to preach in front of the class and then submit myself to the critique of the teacher and the other class members. I received a lot of very positive feedback, but it was all voided by one critical comment the teacher made. I was devastated by that remark. For a week I seriously considered looking for a different job, because my confidence as a preacher was destroyed. Then I asked myself a crucial question: Was the criticism valid? As difficult as it was to admit, I came to the conclusion that it was. As a result I decided to radically change my preaching style, and that became one of the turning points in my career as a pastor.

One of the biblical truths that is part of the statement of faith of almost every evangelical church is that every person is a sinner in need of forgiveness. Jesus Christ is the only sinless person who has ever lived and as such the only person who has ever lived out his life in perfect communion with God the Father. This means that people are fallible, prone to failures and mistakes. It is this reality that brought Jesus Christ into the world in order to pay the penalty for that sin when he died on the cross. Most Christians have no problem accepting that as one of the key doctrinal statements that define our faith experience.

There is, however, a very real problem when we become specific about what that sin looks like. When someone points out a specific sin or a specific way in which we have failed, our natural reaction is to become upset. People don't mind being defined as fallible sinners in broad terms, but they resent being told that they have failed in the specifics. Reality is that we are all redeemed sinners for whom Christ died to pay the penalty for that sin. As a result, we have been forgiven, but reality is that sin is still a part of our lives. We still fail. We still make mistakes. We still sin. We need to learn to live out our common life in our churches in light of this reality.

When we fail to listen to our critics, we fail to take advantage of one of the greatest assets that we have. We need to create an atmosphere in which people feel free to offer their critiques. I don't enjoy being wrong, but because I'm a fallible human being, there are times when I am. It's especially difficult when I'm wrong in a public setting, and church offers me just such a setting.

Worse than being wrong is being wrong in exactly the same way over and over again. The only thing that prevents that from happening is someone telling me that I was wrong the first time. Because the person who corrects me saves me from the embarrassment of repeated mistakes, he is a friend that I cannot do without.

Yet it is important to distinguish among our critics. Not every critic should carry the same weight. Henry Cloud puts it well when he says that "the key is not to count your critics but instead to weigh them."[9] In every church there are people who seem to find something wrong with almost everything. They don't seem to be happy unless they are complaining about some aspect of church life. Then there are other people who are positive and supportive. Often they are the workers who make things happen. When those people are critical about something, we need to make sure that we are listening.

3. CREATE AN AVENUE FOR DIALOGUE

In his best-selling book *Good to Great* Jim Collins looks at the characteristics of companies that moved from being good to great. One of those characteristics was that there was room within the decision-making process for dialogue.

> All the good-to-great companies had a penchant for intense dialogue. Phrases like "loud debate," "heated discussions," and "healthy conflict" peppered the articles and interview transcripts from all the companies. They didn't use discussion as a sham process to let people "have their say" so that they could "buy in" to a predetermined decision. The process was more like a heated scientific debate with people engaged in a search for the best answers.[10]

On the other hand, there are churches that don't allow any discussion at all. One person or a small group of people makes the decisions without input from anyone else. These churches miss out on a lot of valuable input that they could receive if they just gave people an avenue for dialogue.

If leaders are serious about defining reality for their church, they will make sure that there is an avenue for dialogue. Unity should not mean that everyone has to agree on every issue; nor should it mean that members quietly play follow-the-leader without questioning the direction that the leaders are taking.

What would happen in our churches if there were opportunities for people, especially those most affected by a decision, to give input, with the understanding that the leaders would make the decision and the people would support the decision, whatever it was? What would happen if criticism was encouraged by the leaders so that they could hear all the input before making a final decision? What would happen if there was an avenue in which people could express themselves strongly on an issue without being seen as creating disunity? If in business there can be strongly expressed opinions and still a sense of unity within a company, why can't that be the case within our churches, where we have the Holy Spirit to govern our discussions?

I know that this sounds risky, but if we are serious about discovering reality, we need to hear what people have to say, and sometimes that involves hearing things we don't really want to hear.

4. INVITE OUTSIDE INPUT

It's amazing what our conscious mind is able to shut out. I have worn glasses since I was sixteen years of age. For a couple of years I had prescription safety glasses because of my job. In the corner of each lens was a small letter with a circle around it. When I first got the glasses, all I could see was that letter. It almost drove me crazy, but then something amazing happened. My mind was able to ignore that little letter, and I didn't see it at all. I had to be reminded that it was there, because my conscious mind had shut it out completely.

In all of our churches there are the equivalent of those little letters all over the place, things that we no longer see but are evident to every newcomer who attends our services. Usually there are things that need to be fixed around our buildings that we no longer notice. There are elements in our services that are familiar to all the members but make no sense to a visitor. A host of things appear as neon signs to visitors but are invisible to the regular attenders.

If we are serious about defining reality in our church, we may need to see it through the eyes of a newcomer. On occasion, ask someone who is not known to the members to visit on a Sunday morning and then give a report. Give her permission to be completely honest in her findings. If she's worried about sparing your feelings, there will be little value in what she reports. Remember that the truth is always your friend, even when it is hard to take.

My mother once visited a small church for the first time. Being something of an extrovert, she wanted to talk to someone after the service. She decided to just remain in her seat until someone in the congregation came to talk with her. Remember, this was a small enough church that visitors stood out. She sat there until there was only her and the pastor left, and he was putting on his coat to go home. No one spoke with her. No one even seemed to notice that she was there. I imagine that the members would have described themselves as above all else a friendly church, because that's how small churches tend to think of themselves. The strength of a small church is relationships, and few small churches would ever admit that they weren't friendly. The members of that church needed to hear what my mother told everyone outside the church who would listen, because if she had been looking for a new church to attend, she would definitely not have chosen that one.

5. EVALUATE EVERYTHING

"The biggest mistake you can make is not to ask what mistakes you are making."[11] John Maxwell describes that piece of advice as career-changing. It's advice we all need to hear, because in our churches evaluation is something we love to avoid.

Most of us admit quite freely that we are fallible. We acknowledge that only Jesus is infallible. He's the only person in the history of the world who was perfect. We make mistakes. We know that, and yet we hate to submit to evaluation. Doesn't it make sense that when something is planned and carried out by a group of fallible human beings, it should be evaluated? What is the likelihood that a group of fallible sinners is going to get *anything* perfect? Most of us are willing to admit our fallibility in general terms but not in the specifics.

When we fail to evaluate, we condemn people to mediocrity. We never give them the input that will enable them to improve. We are more concerned about making them feel good in the immediate than we are in helping them grow over the long term. A church will never define reality without evaluation.

In most churches, it's not that evaluation never takes place. Whether we like it or not, evaluation happens all the time. The problem is that it takes place over the dinner table after Sunday morning service or when a small group of members get together. It takes place whenever people talk about what they liked or didn't like about a Sunday service or another program in the church. The problem is that their input never gets back to the people involved. That kind of evaluation is destructive, both to the church and to the people. Criticism can only have a positive impact when it's given in a planned, constructive setting in which the people involved are part of the discussion and an atmosphere of trust has been built over time.

A friend attending Bible college was excited about all the new biblical and theological content he was learning, and he wanted to share some of it with others. On several occasions he was given the opportunity to preach in the small church he was attending. The leaders in the church received some negative feedback about his preaching. They decided he wasn't good enough to preach on Sunday mornings and they wouldn't ask him again. No one ever sat down with him and shared their reason for not including him on the preaching schedule. There was never an evaluation time in which he could receive both positive and negative feedback on his preaching. He was just left off the schedule of speakers and left to wonder why.

I've seen this scenario played out time and time again in churches. People in almost every position of ministry have been removed from their positions or just left off a list without a word being said to them. We lose a wonderful opportunity for growth, both for the leadership and the person involved, when we fail to evaluate the person's performance. I feel strongly about this because I've seen so many people hurt in this way. We all need evaluation, but young people who are just starting to discover what God can do through them need it most of all. Sometimes that involves telling them that they aren't gifted in a certain area of ministry, but they should always be told, out of a caring concern for their future growth.

Summary

> When you start with an honest and diligent effort to determine the truth of the situation, the right decisions often become self-evident. Not always, of course, but often. And even if all decisions do not become self-evident one thing is certain: You absolutely cannot make a series of good decisions without first confronting the brutal facts.[12]

Jesus told an interesting story as part of his famous Sermon on the Mount. Two people went out to build a house. The first person built on a solid rock foundation, and whatever stresses came his way, the house stood firm. The second person built his house on a foundation of sand. The same stresses came, and at the height of the storm the house collapsed. I like the way the King James Version expresses it. "*Great was the fall of it*" (Matthew 7:27). Can't you just see it in your mind's eye? This big impressive mansion comes crashing down, and you can hear it fall even over the wind and the rain. It's an unalterable law: the house is only as strong as the foundation upon which it is built.

There are a multitude of programs and strategies available to churches today. There are seminars and books designed to tell us how to grow a church in every way that we might wish to grow it. There are seminars to help us with each individual part of church life. Those seminars can have tremendous value, but they are of secondary importance. Before exploring any changes, we need to make sure that our churches are being built on a solid rock foundation, and that foundation can only be established when we're willing to define reality in our churches. Before we make any change, we need to face the brutal facts about our past, our present and our future. When we've done that, we're ready to plan for the wonderful future that God may have in store for us.

STEP TWO
Intentionally Grow Your Leadership

THREE

The Kind of Leaders Churches Need

I was recently asked by a member of a leadership team in a local church how important I think leadership is. My answer: *"Leadership is everything."* A church will never move beyond the level of its leadership.

A few years ago I was approached by a member of another leadership team who asked for advice concerning the leadership structure in his church. He was convinced that there was something inherently wrong with the structure, but he wasn't sure how to fix it. I assured him that there was nothing intrinsically wrong with the structure. Structure does not cause leadership problems in a church. People cause problems. I had served as the pastor of that church for almost eight years. During the whole of that time the structure had worked extremely well. For a variety of reasons the people had stopped trusting each other, and without mutual trust there was no hope of any structure working.

Let me stress that again. Problems do not lie with the structure. Can structures be improved? Absolutely! Could a different structure work better in your church? Definitely! Are there serious leadership problems because structures aren't working? Never! When a church has leadership issues, the problem always lies with the people involved. Unless the people-problems are solved, the structure will never work.

There are few areas of church life more in need of regular reality checks than leadership. There are at least two reasons for this. The first I have already mentioned. The importance of quality leadership warrants constant checkups. Second, there are few areas in which it is easier for distortions to slip in unawares.

The Need for Self-Leadership

John Maxwell was asked what his greatest challenge as a leader was. He surprised nearly everyone when he responded that his greatest challenge has always been leading himself.[13] I readily concur with what Maxwell said. By far my most difficult task as a leader has been leading myself. There are a number of reasons for this.

As I look back over my life I am amazed at the areas of weakness that I not only didn't acknowledge but didn't even know existed. Every leader needs to constantly self-evaluate.

A few years ago I made a startling discovery. Almost every day I walk four or five kilometres. On those walks I use my time to think. I preach through sermons, plan my writing, work through problems and think my way through countless other issues. Much of the time I'm not even aware that there is anyone or anything around me. My startling discovery was that not everyone uses their time in this way. There are people who simply enjoy the beauty of nature while they walk. There are people who look for other people with whom they can visit. There are people who enjoy the wonder of all the things around them.

By now you're probably shaking your head and asking yourself how I could possibly not have known this. How could I not be aware that for some of you observing the world around you is the highlight of your walk? How could I not understand that a walk isn't really a walk unless you share it with someone else? How could I have thought that everyone becomes lost in his own world while walking like I do? The answer is simple. We all have a tendency to think that the way we do things makes so much sense that of course everyone else does it in just that way.

This illustrates the constant need for self-discovery for every leader. Actually it's been most helpful to have made this discovery because it's made me more aware of what's around me. I still tend to get lost in my own world, but I'm forcing myself to also see more of the world around me and the opportunities for ministry. Our growth as leaders always begins with a commitment to self-leadership.

The people who fill leadership roles in our churches come with a wide variety of different personalities, visions, backgrounds, interests, and training. In fact, just as no two churches are ever exactly alike, no two leaders are alike either. There is no simple formula for making a great leader, but in some areas self-leadership is crucial.

Spiritual Growth

We will never lead people farther than we have gone ourselves. Therefore in a realm that places the highest value on spiritual growth, there is nothing more important for leaders than their own personal walk with God. Leadership ability, experience, and sound judgment are all important, but they can never replace a deep, personal, growing relationship with Jesus Christ.

During his imprisonment in Rome, Paul wrote a letter to the Christians in the city of Philippi. As we read in Acts 16, he planted the church in Philippi and then had to make a quick exit from the city. In this letter, written to his dear children in the faith whom he had to abandon before he could ground them as fully as he would have wished, Paul opened his heart and shared with them his life purpose. This was Paul's reason for living. It was what gave meaning to everything he did.

> *I want to know Christ and the power of his resurrection and the fellowship of sharing in his sufferings, becoming like him in his death, and so, somehow, to attain to the resurrection from the dead.* (Philippians 3:10–11)

As leaders that should be the primary purpose in every one of our lives. We want to know Jesus Christ. Notice that Paul doesn't say that he wants to know more about Jesus. As Gordon Fee points out, this knowledge goes far beyond just head knowledge.

> As verse 10 will clarify, *knowing Christ* does not mean to have head knowledge about him but to know him personally and relationally. Paul has thus taken up the Old Testament theme of knowing God and applied it to Christ. It means to know him as a child and parent know each other, or wife and husband—knowledge based on personal experience and intimate relationship—and thus to know Christ's character intimately.[14]

Knowing Christ in this deep, intimate way is the primary task of every leader. Without that intimate daily walk with Christ, a leader has nothing to give to the church that he leads.

In defining reality in the leadership within our churches the first question that needs to be asked is whether each member of the leadership team has that kind of relationship. What is happening in each person's spiritual journey? Is each leader practicing the spiritual disciplines? Is growth taking place in the leader's life at that particular moment? What are the things that are hindering that kind of growth from happening?

If I could do anything over again in my ministry, I would establish within the leadership team a system of accountability that would enable the leaders to support each other more fully in their spiritual walk. I've been involved in some form of Christian ministry now for almost forty years, and in all that time I've never been asked about my personal devotional life. Throughout my adult life I've had times during which my devotional life has thrived. There have also been times when it was just hanging on by a thread. There have been times of great consistency and times when to say that it was hit and miss might be too generous. Often it has been a struggle, but it has been a struggle that I've had to go through alone.

We hire pastors. We appoint leaders. We assume that because they are pastors and leaders they must have it all together spiritually. We assume, but we probably assume too much. We never actually ask. We never hold each other accountable for our spiritual growth. I want to suggest that this is far too important for us simply to assume. We need to build into our structures some means by which we hold each other accountable and then come alongside each other and give each other the support that we need to thrive in our walk with God.

Over the years of my ministry I have known people in leadership with almost every problem imaginable. I've known people who were undisciplined and thus struggled with any sort of consistency in their devotional life. I've known people who have struggled with addictions to alcohol, pornography, food or tobacco, all of which hindered their spiritual walk. I've known leaders with serious problems in their marriages and families that made it difficult for them to experience a truly vital walk with God. I've known people with a host of other problems, all of which made it difficult if not impossible for them to have a meaningful daily relationship with Jesus Christ. That may sound like a very pessimistic view of leadership, but it is reality. Leaders are people with the same propensity to sin and failure as anyone else in the church.

It's important to note that leaders have the same potential for positive growth as anyone else in the church. I've also worked alongside leaders who were godly men and women with a deep desire to grow in their walk with God. My life has been blessed by those people as I've watched the sacrificial way in which they have served. I've seen the deep love that they have for Jesus Christ and for His people, and I've watched that love in action.

All of us in leadership, though, are human beings. We have been created in God's image and created anew by His Spirit, and out of that comes a great capacity for good. On the other hand, all of us are affected by the fall and live in a sinful world, and that brings with it a capacity for sin. Those two realities exist side by side in all leaders, making accountability and community absolutely essential.

Nothing is more important in our churches than for people to see in their leaders that the Christian life can be real and full of purpose. That only happens when our walk with God touches every part of our everyday life. Richard Foster, who has written a classic on spiritual growth, makes this point.

> We must not be led to believe that the Disciplines are for spiritual giants and hence beyond our reach, or for contemplatives who devote all their time to prayer and meditation. Far from it. God intends the Disciplines of the spiritual life to be for ordinary human beings: people who have jobs, who care for children, who must wash dishes and mow lawns. In fact, the Disciplines are best exercised in the midst of our normal daily activities. If they are to have any transforming effect, the effect must be found in the ordinary junctures of human life: in our relationships with our husband or wife, our brothers and sisters, our friends and neighbors.[15]

That is the primary responsibility of leaders. They are to demonstrate that a person can bring a spiritual vitality into his everyday life. People want to know that their relationship with God can make a difference in the normal living out of their lives. Leaders can only show this if there is that kind of reality in their own lives.

I will say more about the importance of our spiritual walk in a later chapter, but it was important to begin this section on self-leadership at this point. There is a sense in which each leader must take responsibility for her own growth, but that growth happens best in an atmosphere of mutual accountability and caring.

Character Is Everything

> Who a person is will ultimately determine if their brains, talents, competencies, energy, effort, deal-making abilities, and opportunities will succeed.[16]

If churches applied this advice every time they appointed new leaders, there would be far less problems coming out of those appointments. Far too often the appointment of leaders has everything to do with the availability of people or their popularity or business skills or personality or a host of other things and little to do with their character. Whenever we use any criteria other than character we are setting ourselves up for serious problems down the road.

The apostle Paul understood this principle. In outlining the qualities that his young associates were to look for in leaders he focused almost entirely on character traits. He understood that who a person is at the core of his being is far more important than anything they might have done. When Paul instructed Timothy (1 Timothy 3:1—13) and Titus (Titus 1:5—9) to appoint leaders in their respective churches, he understood that character is everything. Even a cursory study of these passages reveals that the qualities he lists are all about character.

One of the most challenging books that I have read in a long time is Dr. Henry Cloud's book entitled *Integrity*. I read it and then a few months later read it again. Then in a few more months, I read it a third time. I was raised to believe that honesty was important. My father was an auctioneer, which meant that I grew up going to auction sales. There was always a point at which my father would have to stop the sale and tell someone that he had just raised his own bid. People would lose track of the bid and think that someone had raised the bid that they had just made. It's just possible that my father was the only person in the place who knew that they had raised their bid, but he always stopped the sale and told them that the bid was theirs. As a young child that made a deep impact on me. My father was known as an honest auctioneer, and much of his business came to him because of that reputation.

Integrity had a huge impact on me, but it was not an easy book to read. The author moved beyond my basic understanding of integrity as simply being the kind of honesty that I had seen in my father and challenged me in areas in which I had never been challenged.

> It is one's make-up as a person in ways much more than ethics alone, that takes people to success or enables them to sustain it if they ever achieve it. While character includes our usual understanding of ethics and integrity, it is much more than that as well. Another way of putting it is that ethical functioning is a part of character, but not all of it. And it certainly is not all of what effects whether someone is successful or becomes a good leader.[17]

If this is true in the world in general it is much more so in the church. It's not enough for leaders to meet the minimum standards of integrity. We need to find leaders who go well beyond the minimum and demonstrate a depth of character that will lead a church through whatever problems it might face.

There have been scores of books written on the subject of leadership, but perhaps the most important leadership principle is one that the apostle Paul came back to again and again. Character is at the heart of good leadership, and character is much more effectively caught than taught. On numerous occasions Paul simply told the people to whom he wrote his letters that they should look at his life and follow his example.[18] He lived out what it means to be a follower of Jesus Christ in such a way that others could see it in practice. He certainly taught those believers every chance that he had, but he realized that for his words to be effective they had to be seen and not just heard.

I know of no more effective test of character for leaders than this one that Paul presents us with. If there are areas of our lives in which we would be hesitant to hold ourselves up as examples to follow, those are the areas in which we need to grow into greater maturity.

I've known many leaders who would respond at this point that they would never offer themselves as an example for others to follow. They know that they haven't arrived yet in their Christian walk, and they don't expect that they ever will this side of heaven. They regard that as the proper response of humility. The problem is that they see their present failures as the norm of Christian living rather than as an incentive to growth. Paul obviously did not agree with this approach, because he exhorted others to follow his example over and over again. As leaders we need to strive for growth so that we can offer our lives, not as the ultimate example of maturity but as people in whom the Holy Spirit is working and producing the character of Jesus Christ. When it comes to character there should be no such thing as a leader who does not have a holy dissatisfaction with his present state and a deep desire to become more like Jesus Christ.

To do justice to the issue of character in leadership I would have to write an entire book on the subject, and even then I would probably just be scratching the surface. I would commend Dr. Cloud's book to anyone who would like to go deeper in examining his own character. It's not an easy book to read in that it will challenge you to go deeper than you might be comfortable in going, but that's what growth in character is all about. We can't grow and remain comfortable at one and the same time. Growth always involves a certain amount of personal pain as we acknowledge our failures. As painful as it might be at times, leaders need to constantly define reality in their own lives so that they can grow and like Paul set an example that others can follow.

Let the Leaders Lead

This may be the most controversial statement that I will make in this book, but I ask that you hear me out before writing me off. If we are to define reality in this area of leadership, it's a very important statement that needs to be made: Most people who hold leadership positions in our churches are not leaders.

Let me repeat that statement.

Most people who hold leadership positions in our churches are not leaders.

It's interesting that this is the way in which God has designed the church. In writing to three different churches Paul talks about the importance of spiritual gifts in the local church.[19] Entire books have been written on this subject, and I am not going to cover the ground that they have already covered, but I do want to make several points that pertain to leadership. The most extensive coverage of this topic is found in 1 Corinthians 12–14, and there are a number of truths that I want to draw out of Paul's teaching in this passage.

1. *There is a variety of different gifts that God has given to the church* (12:4).
2. *Every Christian has been given a spiritual gift* (12:7).
3. *These gifts have been given to benefit the entire church* (12:7).
4. *The Holy Spirit determines which gift each one receives* (12:11).
5. *No one has all of the gifts* (12:27–30).

One final principle is found in Romans 12. Whatever gift we have been given, we are to use it to the best of our ability so that the whole church can be blessed (Romans 12:6–8).

One of the funny and yet somewhat embarrassing moments of my life occurred when I was in my first year of high school. The small school that I attended had limited course selections. In my first two years I had to choose between music and art. I've never been able to sing, but my artistic ability was even worse. I knew that I could get a decent mark on the theory part of the music course, so I took music as the lesser of two evils. Now those who love to sing might object to my calling music an evil, but for someone like myself who can't stay on tune, it has its challenges.

Partway through that first year, the school choir was faced with a problem. There were not enough male voices to balance out the female voices. If the choir was going to reach its potential, this imbalance had to be corrected. The principal decided to take matters into his own hands. He strongly suggested that every male who was taking music as an option should join the choir. Not wanting to jeopardize my future standing as a student, I dutifully obeyed. I went with a friend who sang almost as poorly as I did down to the room where the choir was practicing. We walked into the room right in the middle of one of the songs, took our place among the males, and added our limited talent to the cause.

The choir finished the song, and the leader suggested as nicely as she could that some people in the choir really shouldn't be there and she would encourage them to leave during the next song. I looked at my friend, and we knew that our time as choir members had ended. I think we were part of the choir for less than five minutes. It was at that moment that I had final confirmation that my future would not include singing in a public forum.

Then I had to face the embarrassment of returning to the class that I had left just minutes before, with the whole class knowing that I had been kicked out of the choir. Now, I look back and laugh. I know that the teacher didn't kick me out because she didn't like me or because she wanted to humiliate me in front of the whole class. She asked me to leave because the choir would sound better without me and because she knew that with my lack of ability I would not enjoy the experience. She did it for my good and the good of the entire choir.

At the heart of the whole concept of spiritual gifts is the realization that everyone has not only an area or areas in which she is particularly gifted but also areas in which she is not gifted. Frankly, in most of our churches we need to learn a lesson from my music teacher. There are people who belong in the choir. We need to encourage them to be there. Their voices blend with all the other voices, and the result is beautiful. There are other people who need to be dismissed from the choir because they just don't have the singing ability to be there. They need to find the area in which they have been gifted so that they can know what it is to make a meaningful contribution to the work of the church.

The New Testament mentions more than twenty different spiritual gifts. Among these is the gift of leadership. When we look at the principles previously outlined we see that not everyone has this gift of leadership. The gift is given by the Holy Spirit to a select few within any church body. People who have it are to use that gift to benefit the whole body, just as people with other gifts are to use those for the common good.

This brings me back to the point I made at the beginning of this section: Most people who are in leadership positions in our churches are not leaders. They don't have the gift of leadership and are incapable of providing vision and leadership to the church. They may be an important part of a leadership team, because to be effective a team needs more than just the gift of leadership. Someone with a gift of administration is needed, the person who makes sure that meetings function effectively and things get done. Meetings chaired by someone without this gift are frustrating. Those are the meetings that run until midnight, and at the end of hours of discussion you feel like nothing was accomplished. In some churches, everyone who is part of the leadership team takes a turn chairing the meetings. This insures that at least some of the meetings are going to be ordeals, because they are led by people without any administrative gifts whatsoever. It also contradicts the whole biblical concept of spiritual gifts. If you are currently using this approach, I hope you will abandon it immediately and give the job to the most administratively gifted person on your board.

A leadership team ideally should have someone with a gift of mercy and pastoral care, someone who can bring the personal touch to every issue that's debated. These are the team members who make sure that people's needs are heard and hopefully met.

There should be someone with the gift of wisdom who is able to see potential problems and suggest ways those problems can be avoided. Often she is the quiet person who doesn't say a lot, but when she speaks, her words are full of wisdom.

A leadership team needs all of these people to function well. Not everyone has the gift of leadership, but they may still have an important contribution to make to the leadership team. There does need to be one or two people with the gift of leadership, and just as the administrator needs to administer and those with a pastoral gift need to pastor, those with a leadership gift need to be allowed to lead.

I'm not an advocate of one-person leadership. I believe that the Bible teaches a plurality of leadership, a team all working together, bringing their diversity of gifts into a blended whole. In most of our churches the problem is not one-person leadership. The problem is every-person leadership. We want to apply a standard in the church that we would not apply in any other part of our lives. We have professionals because we recognize the fact that there are areas of our lives in which we are not trained or equipped to do what needs to be done. We go to doctors when we are sick because we understand that they have a wealth of training and experience that allows them to diagnose illness. We go to lawyers because we understand that one needs to go to school to be able to understand the language that is used in legal documents. We hire engineers because we know that there are problems in the construction of buildings that require their skill to solve. My daughter works in the area of environmental studies, with particular expertise in the impact of climate change. I love to ask her environmental questions, but I don't even try to debate issues with her, because I recognize that she knows so much more than I do in this specialized area.

I'm amazed that people who recognize this need for expertise in most areas of life totally ignore it in the church. I've met many people who have absolutely no training whatsoever in any aspect of church life, and yet they are convinced that they know the direction that a church should take. In far too many cases they are so convinced that they are willing to split a church apart in order to get their way.

As part of defining reality within our churches we need to identify those people with the gift of leadership. We need to provide opportunities for these leaders to grow. Then we need to free the leaders up to lead. They need to lead within the framework of a leadership team that is holding them accountable, but we need to let them lead. Those with the gift of administration need to administer. Those with the gift of teaching need to teach. Those with the gift of mercy need to show mercy. Whatever a person's gift is, he needs to be given the freedom to exercise that gift.

If our churches are going to function as God designed them to function, this must also apply to those with the gift of leadership. Those who do not have this gift need to come alongside those who do and encourage and support them in their leadership.

Lifelong Learning

When I was much younger, I had a neighbour who had reached retirement age. She discovered that at that time, as a senior citizen, she could attend university without having to pay tuition. She decided that she would earn a university degree. A few years later she reached her goal. I was too polite to ask her age, but she had to be in her seventies when she graduated. Why did she bother?

Many students who still have their whole lives ahead of them in which to benefit from their studies question the wisdom of university. Why would someone in her retirement years want to do all the work involved in obtaining a degree? I think she believed that learning was a lifelong challenge, and she didn't ever want to stop. I had enormous respect for what she did at the time, and my respect has only grown over the years.

Leadership is a lifelong challenge that none of us ever completely masters. We never know all that we can know about what it means to be a good leader. Leaders come in every size and shape imaginable. Some come into a position of leadership in the church with years of leadership experience in a variety of settings. Other people take on the responsibility with no leadership experience at all. In defining reality in our churches it is important to identify the amount of experience that we bring to a leadership position, but it's also important to realize that whatever experience we may have, we never arrive at a place where we don't have to grow.

I once attended a meeting designed to bring together people who were looking for a church to pastor and churches that were looking for a pastor. It was an interesting experience. On one side of the room was a number of young men who had recently graduated from seminary but had no or very little actual experience in pastoral ministry. On the other side was a group of people representing various churches, all of whom were looking for someone with at least ten years of experience. They were also looking for someone who combined the qualities of Billy Graham, Charles Swindoll and Bill Hybels, all wrapped up in one person. Needless to say, there were not too many matchups made that day.

Most churches want a pastor who has continued to grow in his knowledge and skills. That is as it should be. There are many opportunities available to pastors today to improve their skills. Seminaries offer graduate courses designed specifically for working pastors who want to study at the same time. There are seminars on almost every topic imaginable, and if there aren't seminars, there certainly are books. There's no excuse for any pastor to become stagnant in his ministry.

We seldom ask of our lay leaders what we ask of our pastors. Leadership is a demanding job. Mastering it is a lifelong challenge. There's always something more to learn. Part of what it means to define reality is to identify those areas in which leadership in a church is weak and then determine how to enable the leaders to grow in that area. What would happen if the person on leadership with the administrative gift took at least one course each year that helped him become even more effective? What would a church look like if those with a teaching gift took at least one seminary or Bible college course each year to improve their ability to teach? What impact would it have on a church if those with the gift of mercy or pastoral care took at least one course every year to strengthen their ability in this important area of church life? How much more effective would the leadership be if those with that gift took at least one course each year that would enable them to more effectively cast vision and set direction for the church? Leadership is too important to entrust it to people who aren't growing in their area of giftedness.

Often pastors do not have the gift of leadership. Some pastors are able to envision and empower the people in their churches, but many are not. They bring a lot of other gifts to the mix, but not leadership. They may be excellent teachers. They may have pastoral gifts that enable them to care for their people. They may be evangelists who are able effectively to share their faith. They may have the gift of administration and be able to get things done within their churches. They may have an assortment of gifts, but leadership is not part of the package that they bring to the church.

I read one suggestion that all such pastors should resign. Frankly, that is a very narrow and, I believe, misguided suggestion. There are many pastors who function quite effectively within a church without the gift of leadership. We need excellent teaching. We need pastors who truly love the sheep and are able to care for them when they run into problems. We need pastors who are able to administer the church in such a way that it runs efficiently. I would never encourage a church to fire a pastor just because he isn't a leader.

It is, however, important for every church to identify the strengths and weaknesses of the pastor. A wise church will maximize the pastor's strengths and compensate for the pastor's weaknesses. When the pastor doesn't have a leadership gift—which is probably the majority of cases—the church needs to find others within the church who do have that gift and bring those people alongside the pastor to help create a vision and then lead the church in fulfilling that vision. Pastors who do not have a leadership gift need to recognize that fact and be open to working with others who are leaders. This is not easy for pastors to do. We like to think that we can do everything, but it is a rare pastor who is gifted in all areas of pastoral ministry.

Most of the things that we do as pastors fall into one of four broad areas. First is public communication. This includes preaching and teaching. Second, there are relational parts of the job. This includes pastoral care, counselling, and in many cases evangelism. Third, there are administrative parts of the job, making sure that the church functions effectively. Finally, there are leadership areas, casting vision and empowering people. There is probably not a pastor alive who is strong in all four of those areas.

An important part of defining reality is for a church to identify the pastor's strengths and weaknesses. Then the church needs to encourage the pastor's strengths and compensate for his weaknesses. The difficult part for the pastor is to have the grace to listen to the leaders in his church and admit that he isn't Super Pastor and that he does have weaknesses.

Servant Leadership

There is no more important lesson on the subject of leadership than that found in Paul's letter to the Philippian church. In the second chapter he challenges the people to develop a mindset that emulates that of Jesus Christ, who although He was God did not hold onto the prerogatives of deity but humbled himself and, putting others first, went all the way to the cross for us. With Christ's sacrificial life as our example, Paul challenges the people to put others first. He says that they are not to look out for themselves but rather to put other people's interests ahead of theirs (Philippians 2:1—11).

Leadership in the church is all about putting other people's interests ahead of our own. There's no greater test of leadership than when a leader realizes that a direction she doesn't like is the best direction for the church to go and that she should not only allow it to happen but wholeheartedly support it. Church should never be about having our needs met, and that is especially true for leaders.

Jesus taught that his followers need to live in what has been described as an upside-down world. The values that shape the lives of his disciples are to be the exact opposite of those values that shape the lives of most people in our world. This is especially true in the area of leadership. Politicians strive for power. Business executives are driven to make more money. Athletes and movie stars want more fame. These three things—power, money, and fame—are the motivation behind the success stories that our world praises so highly.

Jesus taught his disciples that their values were to be the exact opposite, and hence the term *upside-down world*. Leadership among his followers was not to be defined by power or money or fame but by the ability to serve. One day, two of Jesus' followers asked if he would grant them a favour. Being a wise leader he asked them to define what the favour was before he would agree to grant it. They replied that they wanted to sit on his right and his left when he came into his Kingdom. This involved a lot more than just a seating arrangement. They were asking that they be chosen for the two most important positions, positions of power and prestige, when Jesus finally took his rightful place as ruler.

Jesus used this as a teaching opportunity. He told them that they were acting as leaders in the world would act, but those weren't the values of his Kingdom. If they wanted to be great in the Kingdom, they needed to learn to serve. In fact, true greatness consisted in being a servant to everyone. Then he drove the point home by reminding them that he didn't come to be served but to serve and to give his life as a ransom (Mark 10:35–45).

It's important to note that this teaching was given to the future leaders of the church, the twelve disciples who in just a few short months would be providing leadership to the church. It is still essential teaching for leaders today.

Courage

Leadership is not about keeping people happy within our churches. This is an important point, because more decisions are made in churches out of fear of people than for any other reason. In congregational churches the ultimate power within the church lies with the membership. Often leaders make decisions that will please the most people because they know if they don't, they could be voted out at the end of their term of service. Sometimes they make decisions that will upset the fewest people in the hope that they will be able to maintain peace within the church. Church fights are never fun. Finally there is the fact that all churches rely on volunteers to run their programs. If people don't like the decisions that are made, they just might stop serving or giving, or worst of all they might leave the church completely.

On some of my more frustrating days I used to dream about what it would be like to be a sergeant in the army. I would give a command, and everyone would run to carry it out. I would be able to tell people what to do and when to do it, and no one would ever dare question my orders. Obviously I wouldn't really want to be in the army, but on days when working with volunteers was most challenging, the thought did seem inviting.

Leadership is about meeting the very real needs that very real people have. It is about growing men and women so that they have a vital relationship with Jesus Christ. To do that, leaders sometimes need to make difficult decisions that people don't necessarily like. It's at those moments when the potential growth of people demands unpopular decisions that leaders truly show what it means to be leaders.

Summary

There are other areas in which self-leadership could be important, but these six will provide a good start. Leaders need to be honest about their own walk with God, and the leadership as a whole needs to create an atmosphere in which they can help each other grow. Character needs to become the primary criterion that churches look for in leaders, and leaders need to be constantly striving for growth in character so that they can provide more effective leadership. Churches need to find those people within their church who are leaders, and then they need to allow those leaders to lead. Leaders need to be committed to lifelong growth. No one has arrived at the point in her leadership skills where she knows all that there is to know. Leadership is putting the needs of the church ahead of our own in each and every situation and leading from a position of servanthood. Finally, leadership requires the courage to lead.

Leadership is a huge challenge. Far too often those of us in leadership positions are not meeting the challenge. We need to be committed to providing our churches with the best leadership possible because a church will never grow beyond the men and women who lead it.

Authority in leadership does not come from the position that a person holds. It comes from the trust that the people have in the leader. Trust is like a bank account into which people make deposits. When that account is full, people give leaders the freedom to lead. They are able to make decisions that people may disagree with but will still support. They are able to move a church forward in the direction that God is calling that church to move.

When the trust account is empty, leaders are given very little freedom to do anything. Decisions are questioned. Direction is challenged. Life becomes difficult for leaders when that freedom to lead is lost. The six qualities outlined in this chapter—spiritual vitality, character, giftedness, growth, servanthood and courage—are the qualities that result in deposits of trust and give leaders the freedom to lead.

STEP THREE
Enthusiastically Embrace Your Uniqueness

FOUR

The Uniqueness of Your Church

As I mentioned in an earlier chapter, my first attempt to pastor was anything but successful. In fact, after three years I was fired. To be perfectly accurate I resigned, but I would have been fired if I hadn't acted first.

The story didn't end there though. In fact, it took an unexpected turn that in my wildest dreams I could never have imagined when I handed in my resignation. It was clear proof that we never know what God has in store for us. Sometimes what looks like an insurmountable barrier can just be a course correction in our walk with God.

A few months after my resignation we were meeting with some close friends who attended the church that we had just left. They made one of the craziest suggestions that I had ever heard. They believed that if we went to the elders, who just a short time before were going to fire me, and suggested that they all resign, I could return as pastor of the church. My friend and I would then form a new leadership team. The really crazy part was that the elders were men in their fifties while we were in our twenties and early thirties. It didn't take much thinking on my part to know that such an idea bordered on sheer insanity. A fired pastor doesn't return to the church that fired him and suggest that he will return if the leadership that fired him will resign. At best they would laugh at me, and I didn't even want to think about what the worst-case scenario might be.

I rejected the idea outright, but my friends didn't quit. They kept returning to the idea each time that we got together. Finally they broke me down, and with great fear and trepidation I agreed to meet with the elders. We set up a meeting with the leadership board and made our outlandish suggestion.

To my utter astonishment, every member of the board agreed to resign and turn the leadership of the church over to us—the pastor whom they had fired and his relatively young and inexperienced friend. As I tried to get my mind around what had happened, I decided to never again limit what God might do.

We decided that we would not attempt to revive the existing church. Instead we shut it down and after a period of a few months reopened it as a brand new church plant. Two of the men who had been part of the previous leadership team stayed with us, and I will always be grateful for the support they gave and the wisdom and experience they so freely shared. The rest of the old leadership team, along with most of the church members, found a new church home elsewhere.

We began with a core of about twenty people. We were a very young church with most of our people in their twenties or early thirties. We wanted to do something new and exciting, something that would set this new church apart from what had been there before. We decided that we would build our vision for the church around creative worship.

Before you read any farther, you need to understand that this took place in the early eighties, before much of what I am about to describe became common practice in churches. If it wasn't completely new, it was certainly different from anything that we had experienced up to that time.

We developed a worship team and began to introduce drama into the Sunday morning services. While keeping some of the old hymns, we introduced praise music. We built our services around a central theme, usually the main point of the sermon. We tried to give people an opportunity to participate verbally in the services. This may seem commonplace today, but then it was revolutionary.

Slowly the church began to grow. With our focus on participatory worship and the use of the arts we began to attract talented young people to the church. It was an exciting time for us all. We felt that we were experimenting, not only with new ways of doing things but with a whole new approach to worship. We were on the cutting edge of what God was doing, and it was a fun, exciting place to be.

Then we were introduced to another new idea. We heard Rick Warren share the story of Saddleback Valley and Bill Hybels talk about Willow Creek. They introduced us to a whole new concept called seeker-driven churches. We had been experiencing slow but steady growth, but here was a chance to move into a whole new level of church growth. We decided that we would abandon our focus on participatory worship and become a seeker-driven church.

There were a lot of things that we already had in place. We used drama in our services. We were already open to new and creative ideas. We didn't have to radically alter our services in order to adapt them to this new approach. A few changes in the preaching style, a little less singing, and definitely a disclaimer before we took up the offering, and we were all set.

I hate to admit it, but once again it didn't work. We had limited success but not amazing growth. There were two basic reasons for this.

First, we didn't understand the concept of a seeker-driven service. We thought that the key to it all was the last part of that phrase. The secret lay in the service. We had visited Willow Creek and experienced their Sunday service. If we could just duplicate that service, we would be all set. We could sit back and watch the people roll in.

We did an amazing job of duplicating the service. We had a drama every Sunday. We had quality musicians performing quality songs. We made the offering disclaimer every week. We had a group of talented young people who were committed to excellence and were willing to sacrifice in order for that to happen.

What we didn't understand was that the service was simply a means by which Willow Creek reached out to people in its community. The key word wasn't *service*. The key word was *seeker*, and we weren't getting any seekers. We were so involved in putting on the services that we weren't spending time with the people for whom we had designed the services in the first place. No matter how good the services were, they couldn't reach people who weren't there, and seekers were a scarce commodity in our services. We didn't have the passion for seekers that people at Willow

Creek had, and no amount of excellence on a Sunday morning could substitute for that passion.

The second problem was that we didn't properly define reality. I praise God for Willow Creek Community Church. I praise him for every person who has come to Christ through their ministry. I thank God for the gift that he has given to the church at large in the person of Bill Hybels. I am grateful for the impact that he has had on my life and on the lives of thousands of other leaders around the world. I rejoice for the way in which Willow Creek has challenged so many of us to renew our focus on seekers who are looking to the church for answers.

But (there is always a "but") we were not Willow Creek, and I was not Bill Hybels. When we changed our focus from participatory worship to seeker-driven services, we moved away from our strengths and tried to build a church around our weaknesses. That was a fatal mistake. We didn't spend time asking ourselves what the reality was, and as a result we failed. We did better than we probably should have and lasted longer than we had any right to last, but the end result was inevitable. An honest look at reality would have prevented it all from happening.

The Danger of Other People's Success

Evangelical churches love to jump on bandwagons. They love fads. That's an awful way to talk about programs that God has used powerfully in specific settings, but I can't think of a better term. The process is repeated over and over again.

A leader develops a new and creative way of doing church. It's usually cutting-edge stuff that no one has ever tried before, and it works. God blesses. Lives are changed. People discover the wonder of the Christian life. As a result, the church grows.

Other churches begin to pay attention. They begin to ask questions. They want to know the secret behind what's happening. They begin to visit the church just to experience something of the Spirit's power that's on display there.

The leadership of the church decides that they need to offer a leadership conference to share what they're doing with a wider group of people. Pastors and church leaders attend the conference and become excited about this new way in which God is working. They return home determined to implement the program in their church setting. Unfortunately, more often than not this new vision for growing the church doesn't work for them.

Usually the people who are putting on the conference understand a basic truth. They realize that what God is doing in their church is unique to their situation. They do their best to share the principles underlying their program, realizing that it's the principles that matter and not how the principles are implemented. I've heard leaders in a number of these conferences state very clearly that leaders should not incorporate what they are doing into a different cultural and geographical setting without a great deal of thought and evaluation. I've heard them clearly outline the dangers of doing so, but people don't seem to hear. Once that dream of their church growing takes hold, they seem to shut everything else out. If it worked in one setting, why can't it work in theirs?

Changes should never be made until a church has run a thorough reality check to see if the proposed changes have any chance of succeeding. Many churches need to change, but those changes need to come out of their own unique world. Rather than looking for a miracle cure in the latest fad, churches need to do the hard work of discovering who God has made them to be and then build change around that.

The following guidelines may help you avoid the danger of leading your church in a direction that is at odds with who God has made you to be.

Discover Your Own Uniqueness

I was walking on a wonderful indoor track that we recently got here in my hometown when someone came up to me and commented on the fact that we were following each other around. Since I not only didn't remember seeing him earlier in the day but didn't remember ever seeing him before, I asked what he meant. He said he had seen me earlier at a retirement home on the other side of a nearby city. When I told him that I had not been there, he replied that I must have an identical twin, because there had been someone who looked just like me at the home. He said that the person had even been wearing an identical coat.

What's amazing is that as much as the person might have thought that I looked like someone else I actually was quite different. In fact, I am different from everyone else in the world. There's only one me, for which many people no doubt are very thankful. God loves variety, and he demonstrated that fact by making every human being a unique person.

He also has made every church to be unique.

For all of my adult life I have been part of the Brethren Church movement. Traditionally churches in that tradition have prided themselves in being patterned after the church in the New Testament. The question that always comes to my mind is, which New Testament church have we patterned ourselves after? I hope that it isn't the church in Corinth, because they had more than their share of problems. They must have given Paul a headache whenever he thought about them, because they blew it at almost every point at which a church could blow it.

Apart from the church in Corinth, there was still incredible variety among New Testament churches. The church in Jerusalem was a megachurch with thousands of members, an unbelievable leadership team, and some serious cultural issues to deal with. The church in Antioch was a cross-cultural church with such a deep concern for the Great Commission that they sent Paul and Barnabas to take the gospel to the Gentile world around them. The church in Philippi was a small church plant with only a tiny handful of people when Paul left them to continue his second missionary journey. The church in Rome was at the centre of the political and military world, in a Latin rather than a Greek cultural setting. Which of those churches should we try to imitate in order to become a New Testament church?

God has made your church unique. It has its own history and culture. It's located in a unique geographical setting. It has its own denominational affiliation. It has its own unique group of members who have their own understanding of what is and is not important in a church. There are a lot of different questions that need to be answered before a church can identify its own uniqueness. Too often a church tries to change before it understands who it already is.

A few years ago I had the privilege of speaking in four completely different church settings over the space of four weeks. The first was the church in which I spent my teenage years, a small-town church that has never had more than forty or fifty members. It was very slow to incorporate change, which meant that it wasn't much different when I visited on this occasion than it was when I attended it about thirty years before. I love that church, because there I received the foundation for my faith. There I was taught the basics, and as much as I have changed over the years, those basic truths are still incredibly important. It was there that I had my first opportunity to serve and there that I preached my first sermon.

The second church was located in the heart of Toronto and consisted of people who spoke Kinyarwanda, the national language of Rwanda in Africa. Most of the people were new to Canada. Many of them had gone through the horrors of the genocide in Rwanda. I preached with a translator, and because most of the people spoke very limited English, I had a hard time communicating one-on-one with them. The worship was amazing, with only a drum to accompany the singing. It was so far removed from the church of my childhood that attending these two on consecutive weekends almost brought with it a serious case of culture shock.

The third church was located in a trailer park on Lake Huron. A friend had a trailer in the park and had been concerned for some time that there was no spiritual influence there. He asked the owners if it would be okay for him to conduct a Sunday service on each of the holiday weekends throughout the summer. On this particular Sunday there were about fifty people in attendance from a wide variety of church backgrounds. Dress was very informal, with shorts and sandals predominating.

The final church was located on a native reserve just south of the Canadian-American border in northern Minnesota. This congregation was in the process of constructing a new building. I asked the man with whom we were staying what advantages the new building would give them over the old one, and he answered that the new one would have indoor plumbing. It was then that I realized that I was no longer in suburban Toronto. This church began with one member and had grown to where there were about twenty to thirty people in attendance. Its location on the reserve carried with it certain challenges that were different from anything that I had faced in my church experience.

During that four-week period I also attended but didn't speak at a large urban church with four services accommodating about fifteen hundred people. A highly skilled worship team led contemporary praise songs. Multiple staff offered a wide variety of programs for every age and preference. There was a beautiful new sanctuary with all the technical advantages that any church could want. The pastor was a powerful preacher. Every part of the service was done with excellence.

Five very different churches in five very different locations built around five very different cultures. Attending those churches in a four-week span impressed on me the reality that God is not in the business of making cookie-cutter churches. In fact, he does just the opposite. He creates every church to be completely unique, completely different, and it's important that we identify and appreciate that uniqueness in our own church.

Perhaps no one understands the uniqueness in churches more than Lyle Schaller. He wrote an excellent book several decades ago entitled *Looking in the Mirror: Self-Appraisal in the Local Church*. This is well worth reading. It will give you some ways of looking at your uniqueness that you probably haven't thought of. For instance, he divides churches into seven different categories based on size. In his unique style he classifies them as cats, collies, gardens, houses, mansions, ranches and nations. He then expands on these analogies to outline the characteristics that make each size church unique from the others.[20]

Appreciate the Positives in Every New Movement

Over the course of a few months two different members of the same church expressed the same basic concern about the direction that their church might take. With great emotion in his voice the first person asked me if the church was going to become a seeker-driven church. I explained that there is very little danger of that happening. The church is so far from being seeker driven that there's no danger of it adopting that model.

A second person expressed with the same level of emotion the concern that they might become part of the emerging church movement. My reaction once again was that there's little danger of that ever happening. First, I'm not sure that the person understood what the emerging church is, and second, the values that the emerging church would espouse are very far from the values of that church.

What concerned me in both of these cases is that these movements were seen as dangers that the church needed to avoid. They were at best corrupting influences that could bring harm to the church and at worst evils that needed to be avoided at all costs.

Churches tend to go to one of two extremes. The first is what I have just described. When something new comes along, it's seen as a danger to avoid. People on this side of the spectrum tend to look for the problems in each new movement, and when they find those problems, they condemn the movement outright.

The second response is total acceptance. People in these churches are looking for the secret to growth, and they are willing to latch on to anything that promises results. They buy the books, attend the conferences and implement the programs with the hope that this will be the magic formula for success.

The best approach is to avoid both of these extremes. As is usually the case, the best response is found in striking a balance somewhere in the middle. A whole library of books could be written on the importance of balance in the Christian life, and once again it is the answer here. To condemn something new without looking for the positive in it strikes me as the height of foolishness. On the other hand, to wholeheartedly accept something new as the answer to all the problems in our churches is foolishness as well. When we do that, we fail to take into consideration our own uniqueness as a church.

Over the course of my life I have seen a lot of new movements come and go. It's harder to get excited about something new when you are older, because you've seen too many new ideas. The best sellers of one time period can often be found in the bargain bin a few years later. One of the most common mistakes that the leaders of these new movements make is to think that what they are espousing is God's answer to everything that is wrong in the church rather than part of the ongoing work that God is doing and has been doing all down through the centuries.

In the 1970s I was introduced to Ray Stedman's book *Body Life*. He recaptured the concept of spiritual gifts and every-member ministry within the Body of Christ. For centuries real ministry had been reserved for a select group of people called clergy. Through Body Life services Stedman opened up ministry within the body to everyone. It was a revolutionary concept at that time.

In the 1980s I heard about Willow Creek Community Church and the ministry of Bill Hybels. He introduced the idea that seekers really matter to God. Jesus called his disciples to be fishers of men because he cared about the people for whom the disciples would be fishing. They were important. Willow Creek placed a high priority on reaching those seekers.

In the 1990s I read Rick Warren's book *The Purpose Driven Church*. He suggested that the church should have a purpose. God didn't intend for His church to wonder aimlessly with no reason for its existence. He suggested that the starting point for every church should be the question "Why do we exist?" When a church has identified its reason for being, everything else can flow out of that.

In the past decade attention has been paid to the emerging church. I was introduced to the writings of Brian McLaren. Brian challenged the church to take a hard look at the cultural changes that are taking place in our Western society and to ask ourselves what it means to be relevant in light of the major cultural shift from a modern to a postmodern world.

I have used these four examples because for me they encapsulate the four decades of my adult life. I haven't agreed completely with any of them, but each one was built around a truth that the church needed to recapture. Ray Stedman taught us that for a church to be all that it is meant to be, every member needs to be actively involved in ministering to the other members. Bill Hybels reminded us that seekers are important to God and they should be important to us as well. Rick Warren showed us that we need to understand the purpose of the church and then build all that we do around that purpose. Brian McLaren taught us that in a changing world we need to find a way to communicate truth that is effective and relevant to those around us.

God is constantly using men and women to recapture truths that are important for the church at a particular point in history. As we look at the latest new approach to church that has captured the interest of people, we need to ask ourselves what it is in this new teaching that God wants us to grasp. We don't have to accept an approach in its totality in order to benefit from the truth that it is recapturing, but we don't want to reject it in its totality and not benefit from it at all. The secret is to identify the key principle that is being taught and apply it to your church without sacrificing those things that make your church unique.

Settle for Consistent Rather Than Spectacular

I no longer read books with the hope that I will be overwhelmed by the material the author shares. Now I hope that I will get one or, if I'm lucky, two new concepts that will challenge me to think in a new way. A couple of years ago I was reading a book entitled *Historical Drift*. It was written by Arnold L. Cook, past president of the Christian and Missionary Alliance in Canada. Cook quotes something that Jim Collins said at a leadership conference sponsored by Willow Creek Community Church. "A charismatic leader is not an asset but a problem to recover from."[21]

Cook says that Collins shocked his audience at the conference with that statement. For me it was more than mere shock. I was dumbfounded as the truth of what Collins said sank into my mind. All my life I had been led to believe that it was the charismatic person who was the ideal leader. He was the one who could move mountains and bring spectacular growth to a church. Now I was being told that rather than being an asset, he is probably going to turn out to be a problem.

As I looked back over my own church experience I had to admit that what Collins said was true. I had been involved with some charismatic type leaders, and without exception over the long haul they had created far more problems than they had solved. When I looked at many of the churches that had experienced sustained growth, the pastor was not a charismatic leader. He was a consistent, steady leader committed to the long-term health of the church.

If I could give one piece of advice to every search committee in every church looking for a pastor it would be this: Don't look for the short-term solution to your church's problems. Look for the person who is going to bring good but steady leadership over the long haul.

Along with millions of other people across Canada and the United States, one of my goals for this year is to lose a considerable amount of weight. So with weight loss on my mind I typed "fad diets" into my computer and hit the search button. A couple of seconds later I was informed that there were 1,700,000 sites from which to choose. I discovered that there is a fad diet to suit every taste. If you want to build your diet around a specific type of food you can choose among grape, raw food, cabbage soup, red wine, peanut butter, pizza, ice cream, grapefruit, bread and butter, or chicken soup diets. If you like exotic locals, there are the Mediterranean, South Beach, Cambridge, Hollywood and Beverly Hills diets. If time is of the essence you can pick between a one, three, seven or twenty-one day diet. I only looked at a few sites. I'm sure that the options are endless.

Anyone who is serious about losing weight understands an important principle. We gain weight as the result of bad lifestyle choices over time. The only effective way to lose weight is through good lifestyle choices over time. The quick way is almost never the best way.

This same principle holds true in our churches. Whether we are choosing a new pastor or buying into a new program, slow, consistent growth is what we need. In some very rare cases God produces spectacular growth. It happened on the Day of Pentecost in Jerusalem when Peter preached his first sermon. It has happened down through the centuries and is still happening in some settings today, but we need to understand that these are exceptions rather than the rule.

Even in the New Testament, spectacular growth was the exception. When Paul preached his sermon on Mars Hill in Athens (Acts 17) he didn't get the kind of results that Peter did when he preached in Jerusalem. When Paul left the little group of believers in Philippi, they were just that, a tiny church plant with a handful of members.

I'm not suggesting that we should settle for mediocrity in our churches. I do believe though that consistent growth over time is far better than a spectacular but short-lived burst of growth that often leaves a church with more problems than it had before. Fireworks are spectacular, but they're gone in a few seconds. To cook a good meal requires consistent heat over time.

Summary

So how should you approach the wide selection of possible new approaches to church growth that fills the bookstores? First, discover what makes you unique. You are different from every other church in existence, and it's important that you understand that uniqueness before you start looking at other options.

Second, discover the positive in all the options that are out there, and then ask how you can apply those positives to your unique situation.

Third, look for the options that provide consistent growth over time rather than those that advocate spectacular growth right away. Whether you are choosing a new pastor or a new program, the charismatic option is not an asset but a problem to recover from.

FIVE

The Uniqueness of the Small Church

While mega-churches and their leaders continue to receive most of the attention in the church world, numerically the small church still dominates the ecclesiastical landscape in Canada and the United States. A survey conducted by Outreach Canada in 2003 determined that 77 percent of Protestant churches and 73 percent of evangelical churches in Canada averaged less than 150 in Sunday morning attendance.[22] Lyle Schaller states that more than 73 percent of churches in North America have fewer than 175 in attendance.[23] Other writers quote slightly different figures, but all agree that there are more small churches than all other size churches put together. The fact that there are so many should mean that they are a priority for anyone working in the North American church scene.

Personally, I have been involved in small churches all of my life. I spent my childhood and teenage years in two small churches in Northern Ontario. I have been part of three church plants and have served as the pastor of small churches. I have worked with small-church leaders and have had my share of successes and failures within the small-church setting. What I share in this chapter is not written as an academic exercise but as a love story in that over the years I have fallen in love with the small church. I have attended large churches at various points in my life and value the work that they do, but my passion is for the small church with all of its unique strengths and frustrations.

Defining the Small Church

Any attempt to find agreement on a definition of the small church on the basis of numbers will fail. Different authors choose different numerical parameters, but any attempt to provide a numerical definition is arbitrary. Why does a church suddenly cease to be a small church simply because it reaches a certain numerical standard?

The small church is defined more by what it is than by the number of people who attend on a Sunday morning. Those who have studied the small church have used a variety of analogies in an attempt to capture something of what is at the heart of the small church, and all have the same focus. The small church is built around relationships.

Steve Burt compares the small church to an extended family.[24] At the heart of any family are relationships. Carl Dudley talks about the small church as a primary group, which he then defines in terms of relationships.[25] Anthony Pappas compares the small church to a folk society and then stresses the importance of relationships.

> The significant reality in small-church society, the reality that motivates behavior and organizes life, as profit is to business and knowledge is to science, is not things or ideas. It is not even people per se. It is the relationships between people. Of course, individual people are necessary if interpersonal relationships are to occur, but individualism is not the significant reality of the small church. How we are connected and placed in a personal world, the movements within our social world, how we are rooted and placed among those who we think of as "us"—this is the focus of small-church concern. This is the small church world.[26]

Without an appreciation that relationships are absolutely essential to our understanding of the small church, any definition that we might develop will be incomplete. Defining the small church then is much more than just a matter of numbers. Rather it is about the quality of church life that is found in the small church. For this reason almost everyone who has studied small churches agrees that they are very different from the medium-sized or large church. David Ray captures this well:

I have two fundamental convictions about small churches. First, they are the right size to be all that God calls a church to be. They are not premature, illegitimate, malnourished, or incomplete versions of "real" churches. Second, they are a different breed of church. A small church is as different from a large church as a Pekingese is from a Saint Bernard. They look, feel, think, and act differently. Differences in size yield crucial differences in form and function. Ministry, not in tune with and tailored to these churches' differences in size, is doomed to failure.[27]

While the small church is different from middle-sized or large churches, there is a striking similarity between small churches regardless of location. A small Baptist church in Northern Ontario probably has more in common with a small Pentecostal church in Alberta than it does with a large Baptist church in the next town.

These two elements in our understanding of the small church—the importance of relationships and the uniqueness of the small church as compared to large churches—should help to shape the church's thinking in very practical terms. The importance of relationships means that all the programs within a small church must be relational. When the small church attempts to build on any other foundation, it builds on its weaknesses rather than its strengths. The temptation for small-church leaders is to try to build on a mega-church foundation, which is almost guaranteed to fail. I shared my own experience with attempting to do this in the previous chapter, so this caution comes out of the lessons learned from that failure.

In my early days of pastoral ministry I attended a Billy Graham School of Evangelism in Boston. It was an amazing experience to be in a hotel with hundreds of other pastors learning from men and women who had been blessed by God in their ministries. Every evening we traveled to the stadium where the old Boston Braves used to play baseball. For a fan of sports history, just to be in that stadium, where baseball history had been made, was a thrill. To see scores of people respond to the invitation was an even greater thrill. I do remember though at one of the sessions thinking of the contrast that existed between most of the pastors who were there and the speakers who were doing the teaching. I wasn't able to ask everyone where they came from, but I imagine that the majority of the pastors were from small churches, just like I was. All of the speakers were either members of the Billy Graham Association or leaders of mega-churches from across the United States. Even back then I wondered to what degree the messages delivered by mega-church pastors related to the small church pastors who were hearing those messages. We were being taught ways in which God was working in large churches, but did those large-church methods apply to the small churches that most of the pastors were trying to lead? At the heart of what was being taught was a belief that the small churches represented were simply smaller versions of the large churches represented by the speakers. I would have loved to have heard how small churches were making an impact, but in a church culture that honours bigness, that was not likely to happen.

Characteristics of the Small Church

While there is general agreement that the small church is uniquely different from larger churches, there is very little agreement regarding the qualities that define that uniqueness. One author gives ten characteristics of a small church.[28] Another outlines twenty-six characteristics.[29] Still another lists fifteen.[30] Realizing the impossibility of developing a definitive list of small-church characteristics, I'll present three that have particular application to small-church life.

The small church is relational. This has already been emphasized, but it needs to be noted again because it is the most important characteristic of the small church. Everything—worship, evangelism, discipleship, teaching, and more—needs to revolve around this fact. The small church is relational.

I once attended services in two very different churches on consecutive Sundays. The first was a large-city church with more than 1,500 people attending four different services on Saturday evening and Sunday morning. The other was a small-town church that averaged less than 100 people at their one service on Sunday morning. It just happened that both churches were holding a baby dedication. At the large church about ten babies were being dedicated. A worship team led the congregation in singing while the dedication was taking place. There was a staff person at the end of each aisle, and each couple took their child forward to one of the staff members. Only the parents went forward, and only those involved and the people in the seats right beside them were able to hear what was being said. In a short time all of the babies were dedicated, and they were able to move on with the remainder of the service. It was very efficient and very professional, but it seriously lacked the personal touch.

In the small church the next week the pastor invited the parents of the only child being dedicated to join him at the front of the auditorium. He then invited the grandparents to come forward as well. Then on the spur of the moment he decided to include any close friends sitting in the audience, and finally he announced that since they were all part of this couple's spiritual family, anyone who wished to could join them at the front. By this time there were about twenty people gathered around the couple. The dedication took place, and then family, friends, and everyone else who was at the front hugged this couple and congratulated them on the step they had taken. It wasn't very professional, but it sure was personal. The pastor of that church understood that in the small church it's all about relationships. Having all those people around them was more important to the couple than having a finely crafted service.

A second characteristic of the small church is that it is intergenerational. There aren't enough people attending the church to provide appropriate age-related programs for every group in the church. As a result, most of the activities are open to every age group. Adults know the names of most of the children in the church. Seniors may speak to teenagers. Social activities may include all age groups, so that young parents are mingling with older adults who have experienced the challenges of parenthood and survived. Anthony Pappas stresses the importance of the personal nature of the small church:

> Small churches have a future. The personal nature of the small church is its divine gift to humanity. In the small church each person is important, each person can make a difference to

someone else, each person can experience unconditional love, each person is called to live up to his or her potential, each person is of infinite worth. The people-oriented qualities of small-church life make it necessary to each generation.[31]

The interpersonal connections within the small church that Pappas describes as its greatest strength become even more significant when applied to the intergenerational aspect of the church. The pastor may be on a first-name basis with the teenagers. The leadership should be able to call each child by his or her first name.

One of the greatest tributes to a church leader that I have ever heard came from a group of teenagers who were trying to decide how to move forward with some plans. After considerable discussion, one of the young people suggested that they ask one of the leaders, identifying him by name. There was unanimous support for that suggestion, and then the young person gave the reason. She simply said, "He loves us." That kind of tribute can come only in a setting in which the leadership has considerable interaction with the youth.

As I will expand on in a later chapter, the challenge of the Great Commission is to make disciples. Two aspects of the intergenerational nature of the small church contribute significantly to this process: example and involvement. Because so many of the activities are intergenerational, the potential for exposing children and teenagers to the example of older, mature Christians is greater. There is certainly more opportunity for involvement on the part of younger people. They are able to participate in worship, Sunday school, youth leadership and other activities in which the expectation for excellence is lower. They can attempt things knowing that there will be a high level of forgiveness for mistakes. Discipleship necessitates participation and requires involvement in ministry, even for teenagers. Loren B. Mead notes that this higher level of participation results in leadership development. Many of the people currently serving in leadership in all sizes of churches come out of smaller churches:

> One of the greatest gifts that small congregations have to give is effective Christians. Many of the denominational bodies, as

well as the city and suburban churches, are deeply indebted to the leadership they have received from members whose early nurture in the faith was carried out in small congregations. Everywhere I go across the country, I find leadership in larger congregations disproportionately borne by those who were nurtured in small congregations. Frequently the smaller-membership congregation is not even aware of the power of this exporting of resources, and almost never is the larger church aware of it. The fact remains, however, that smaller congregations produce a larger share of the key lay persons and members that have in several generations produced five to eight young people who grew up, left home and became key figures in churches elsewhere, not always of the same denomination. These are extraordinary gifts.[32]

A third characteristic of the small church is a distinctive relationship between the pastor and the members. Carl Dudley has captured the essence of what most small churches are looking for in a pastor:

The small church cannot afford a specialist and is not primarily interested in measuring success based on program activity. The small church is built around the relationships of people to people. They want to know the pastor as a person first. Only second are they interested in the pastor's skills. Members of the small church want from their pastor what they find most satisfying in belonging to the small church; they aren't primarily interested in the specialist or the generalist. The small church wants *a lover*.[33]

This is far removed from the advice given by many today who see the primary role of the pastor as leading his church to become a large church. These advisors would suggest that the primary responsibility of a pastor is not to love his people but to lead them to experience numerical growth. The leader of a large church is very limited in the amount of time that he is able to invest into individual members, and the larger the church, the less the available time. In a mega-church someone could attend the church for years without ever meeting the senior pastor. To suggest that this should be the approach of the pastor of a small church in order to create a structure in which future growth can occur is to ignore the greatest strength that the small church has.

Loving the people within the church and providing leadership at the same time is an extremely difficult balance for a pastor to achieve. The pastor who tries to impose standards of leadership that are foreign to the small church is ultimately going to fail. On the other hand, the pastor who does a great job of loving the people but doesn't provide any direction for them is going to fail as well.

Every seminary program, designed to prepare young pastors for ministry, needs to include a strong emphasis on both love and patience. A full course on both might be appropriate. While it may not have the appeal of a course on the missional church or on preaching, it might prove to be more important in the success of a small-church pastor than anything else.

The small church is different and as such has unique qualities that characterize it. It has great future potential if it plans around such characteristics as its relational nature, its intergenerational nature, and the unique relationship between the pastor and the congregation.

A Biblical Perspective

A biblical perspective of the small church is needed in order to appreciate its full value. Often it's suggested that there's something unbiblical about a small church because it isn't growing as fast as other churches. Peter Wagner uses the example of the church in Jerusalem to make this point:

> A model church in the New Testament is the one in Jerusalem which was founded on the day of Pentecost. On that one day the nucleus of 120 added 3,000 new members. They were baptized, they grew in their understanding of Christian doctrine, they worshipped together regularly, they developed fellowship groups, they shared their material goods with one another, they

exercised their spiritual gifts. As a result the church continued to grow and "the Lord added to the church daily those who were being saved" (Acts 2:47). This was a healthy church. And one characteristic of healthy churches is that they grow.[34]

While recognizing the amazing work of God that took place on that day, I question whether the Jerusalem church is the most appropriate example for all other churches throughout the centuries. After all, were there not unique factors at play on that particular day, factors that cannot be duplicated in any other setting? Jesus had just died. Some of the people listening to Peter on that day were eyewitnesses to his death. There were rumours of Jesus' resurrection circulating around Jerusalem. Many had witnessed some aspect of his three-year ministry. The leaders of the church were a group of men who had just spent three years with Jesus. These are all historic factors that will never be repeated. It's not right to hold every other church in history to the standard of the Jerusalem church. The growth in that church came out of a very unique set of circumstances.

Also, why should that church be chosen as opposed to the other churches described in the book of Acts? Why is the Jerusalem church the example rather than the Antioch church or the Colossian church? They were not simply replicas of the church in Jerusalem. There was great diversity among churches in the first century. When Paul left cities such as Thessalonica and Philippi, the churches were quite small. We don't have any knowledge of their subsequent growth, and to suggest that they became large goes beyond what the Bible states. The diversity of churches in the New Testament suggests that there is not one "right" size church.

The New Testament authors used a number of different pictures to describe the church. Each one adds something to our understanding of what the church is supposed to be. Paul compared the church to the human body (1 Corinthians 12:3). He also used the picture of a building, with each member being a building block (Ephesians 2:20–22). He compared the church to a bride for whom Christ sacrificially gave his life (Ephesians 5:25–33). Peter described the church as the people of God (1 Peter 2:9). None of these pictures has anything to do with size. What matters is not how large a church is but the relationship between the members of the body and the head, between the building blocks and the cornerstone, between the groom and the bride, between the people and the One to whom they belong.

Ultimately the church derives its value not from the number of people that attend on a Sunday morning but from the relationship that the church has with the One who is the centre of all that the church is and does. E. Stanley Jones expresses this powerfully:

> In the person of Jesus Christ the Christian church holds within itself a motive and power that does produce changed character. So Jesus Christ is the center of worth and hope of the Christian church. We have this treasure in an earthen vessel. Don't point to the earthen vessel—its cracks, its outworn inscriptions, its outworn shape, its unmodern appearance, but rather look at what it holds. It holds the person of Jesus Christ. As long as it holds him, it holds the most precious, the most potent, and the most present value that this universe holds, barring none.[35]

There is so much truth in what E. Stanley Jones says. The value isn't found in the vessel. It's found in the One whom the vessel holds. Whether that vessel is a mega-church with thousands of people attending or a small church with only a handful of members, the value does not come from the vessel. The value comes from the One within the vessel, Jesus Christ.

Small churches struggle with a shortage of resources—workers, finances, space, gifted people—all realities that make life difficult. If the congregants only look at the externals, they can become overwhelmed by what they don't have. They need to be encouraged to focus on what they do have, and at the very top of that list of blessings is the constant presence of Jesus Christ in his church.

Jesus himself put the value of the small church in perspective when he said, "*Where two or three come together in my name, there am I with them*" (Matthew 18:20). The presence of Jesus whenever and wherever his people gather is what ultimately gives meaning to the church. Jesus did not say that he was only present when two or three hundred gathered, much less two or three thousand. He is present even when there are only two or three people who meet in his name. Nothing could give greater value to the small church than that promise.

The Impact of the Small Church

In writing my thesis for the doctor of ministry program, I conducted interviews with six small churches on the subject of evangelism. I interviewed at least two members of the leadership at each church, and then I interviewed someone who had come to faith in Jesus Christ through the ministry of that church and was continuing as an active participant. Those were exciting stories to hear, for two reasons. The first was that I was hearing how people's lives had been powerfully changed by the impact of the gospel. The second was to hear how small churches were being used by God to impact their communities. I'm going to share those six stories in the hope that they will plant a seed in your small church as to what God can do when you become involved in people's lives.

STORY ONE

The first interview took place at Pinewoods Gospel Chapel in the town of Angus in Southern Ontario. The town is located right beside a military base, which has a huge impact on the town. The current pastor arrived at Pinewoods in 2007, and since that time the church has undergone a major transition in their understanding of and their approach to evangelism. They have become much more involved in the community, with the goal of being Christ's hands and feet in Angus.

The interview at Pinewoods was with a husband and wife. Their two stories were so intertwined that it made sense to interview them together. The husband was raised in a family in which there was no church involvement. He described himself as having no faith and believing that because of the sin in his life he couldn't come to God. His original connection with the church came out of wanting to please his wife, who had some contact and wanted to attend on a more regular basis.

The wife grew up in a Roman Catholic family in which the father professed a strong faith in the church but at the same time abused the children. When she left home to attend university, she also left the church. Through a series of very difficult experiences she began to renew her interest in the church. She attempted to return to a Roman Catholic church, but the priest was too busy to talk with her. Through a connection with a friend she found her way to Pinewoods. She had several encounters with people there before she started attending the church with regularity. During that time, the people at Pinewoods helped the family in very practical ways.

Both the husband and wife stressed the importance of the relationships in their coming to faith within the context of Pinewoods. When confronted with the possibility of leaving Angus, the wife stressed that the deciding factor was the place that Pinewoods had come to have in their lives.

> "I said that I really liked Pinewoods. I'm sticking to Pinewoods. I'm not leaving Pinewoods. Better than the family that I have ever had because they just engulf you with love and acceptance and forgiveness. They definitely walk with Jesus here."[36]

When asked if only the leadership practiced this kind of love and acceptance, they said that it began with the leadership but was "leadership that leaked through the lines." That's a good description of the leadership at Pinewoods Gospel Chapel and its impact on the church as a whole.

STORY TWO

Elmvale Community Church started as a traditional Brethren Assembly and has undergone a significant transformation over the past five or six years. In those early years most of the members commuted from outside the town itself. There were about seventy people involved in the church, but not more than a dozen were community people. When the current leadership realized this, it was the spark that ignited a desire to change. A desire to become more community-focused and to provide answers that couldn't be found in a traditional approach resulted in a new direction for the church. Elmvale today has a very real desire to make a difference in the lives of the people who live in their community.

The interview at Elmvale was with a woman who grew up with only minimal church exposure. She attended a United church a few times with her grandfather, which was largely a positive experience for her. She also attended a Roman Catholic church once with a girlfriend, which, because of the strangeness of the setting, was a very negative experience. She came out of a difficult background filled with alcoholism and abuse. After the birth of one of her children she went through a period of depression, which resulted in her being hospitalized. At the most difficult point of her stay in the hospital she cried out to God for help. She said if God would help her, she would go to the little church up the road, which was Elmvale Community Church.

On her first Sunday out of the hospital, she and her husband attended the church for the first time. The pastor and his wife invited them home for lunch, and during the afternoon she told them her whole story. In describing that first meeting and its impact on her life, she said that she felt accepted by the church and particularly by the pastor and his wife. She said it felt comfortable and like they were friends from the beginning. She now describes the church as her family and considers herself closer to them than even to the members of her own family. The relational aspect was very important to her journey to faith.

While she was quite clear as to exactly when her commitment to faith in Christ took place, she described it as part of a process that continues on in growth that is taking place day-by-day now. She described the process as something pulling her.

> "I did feel after being in hospital that something existed. I wouldn't have said Jesus or the gospel as I would now, but there was something, and every time I went I felt like I was a step closer to realizing what that was. Every time I went to a small group or attended a church function, I felt like I was going the right way. Something was pulling me that way."[37]

THE UNIQUENESS OF THE SMALL CHURCH

The church was willing to give her the time she needed to be pulled by the Holy Spirit into a commitment of faith. Having just come from the hospital, in her own words she was "not the most put-together person" on her first visit to the church. From that very uncertain beginning she has developed into a growing, serving, giving member of the church.

While the interview was only with the wife, her husband has also come to faith, so they are now both involved in the church and growing in their walk with God.

STORY THREE

In 1970 Bridletowne Park Church began meeting in a school in the northeast corner of Toronto. It was a church plant with the Associated Gospel Churches. Shortly after, a Christian developer donated land in a new subdivision to the church, and at the same time they also received a generous donation of money from a church that had closed down and sold their building. In 1973 they moved into a new building at their present location. The two donations contributed to a feeling that God has placed them in their location and has a purpose for them being there.

In the forty years since that beginning, the community around the church has undergone radical changes. In 1970 this part of Toronto was primarily a white Anglo-Saxon community. Today there is a very diverse population, with the two largest groups being Chinese people from Mainland China and Tamils from Sri Lanka. As a result, the church began to feel very disconnected from the community. The past ten years have been about finding out if God has a way forward for the church in that community. The challenge has been to see how they can be relevant to newcomers to Canada. As a result, the church today is much more ethnically diverse in its makeup and much more engaged with people who live in the neighbourhood.

The new believer I interviewed is a recent immigrant to Canada, a young woman who came from China in 2005. When she came here, she had no understanding of the Christian faith whatsoever. Shortly after arriving she met with a friend she had known in China, who invited her and her husband to a Mandarin-speaking church in Toronto. For about three years she attended sporadically, always at the invitation of her friend. In 2008 she became pregnant, and the realization that she was carrying a new life inside her greatly increased her interest in God. She began attending with much greater regularity. During this period she made the decision to become a Christian. Shortly after, another friend invited her to attend Bridletowne Park, describing the church as "very nice, very warm, like a family."

While only the woman was interviewed, she made it very clear that her husband was the leader in this spiritual journey. Even as a child back in China he had had an interest in God. He also came to faith during this time, and she was grateful that he was very much a part of this process.

The ethnic diversity in the church and the willingness of Bridletowne Park to adapt to the new reality in their neighbourhood was very important to her.

> "Here people are different. I like this difference. God is bringing people from all the nations, from different parts of the world together. He's going to surprise me with so many different people in the church. And it is very interesting to see all the different people's reaction in the church. They wear different dress. Everything is different, and I like that."[38]

STORY FOUR

The Rock Community Church is also part of the Associated Gospel Churches of Canada. It's located in Woodstock, Ontario, a city of about 35,000 people. It began as a house church and over its history went through several church splits, which seriously affected its growth.

In 1992 the church carried out a building program and was able to erect a building that was much larger than their immediate needs. It was built in a new subdivision with the hope that people would be attracted to it. Shortly after, there was a major split, which reduced numbers even more. According to a current leadership team member who went through that period, while they built the church with the hope of attracting new people, they refused to change the mindset that had failed to attract people in the past.

After a period of struggling along on their own, they were offered help from the denomination, which designated the church as a restart and gave it almost the same status as a church plant. So even though they have a history, much of their time and energy over the past couple of years has been devoted to building up an operational structure. Attendance ranges between sixty and eighty people on a normal Sunday.

The interview was with a man in his mid-thirties who lives just outside the city. He and his significant other came to the Rock without any previous contact with the church or anyone in the church. He grew up in a Roman Catholic family in London and like many young people became involved in the party scene in high school. This continued after he left home, until alcohol and drugs were controlling his life. In his own words, "There was no further that I could go down in life other than death." Realizing this, he moved back to London and began to get his life in order. He met his girlfriend, who had been raised in a family with a strong Christian commitment. After moving to Woodstock, she decided she wanted to go back to church, and he was willing to accompany her.

He has been influenced by the kindness and love of the people at the Rock. He broke his wrist and was unable to keep up with the work on his horse farm. At the same time his girlfriend was trampled by one of the horses and broke her back, so she also was unable to work. Very quickly they began to fall behind in the upkeep of the farm. One Saturday morning twelve people showed up at their farm, asking what they could do to help. By the end of the day almost everything was done that needed to be done. The couple had never experienced anything like this before and were amazed that people they hardly knew would help them.

"I come from a background where you can live right beside somebody, neighbours, and never say hello. You don't even know who they are, first or last names, and you could live there for five years. People can just go to a building, a church, and have a strong belief, and they're over at my place pulling weeds when they've only met me once or they haven't met me. That's a pretty amazing thing in human nature. When acts like that can be achieved you got to say there's more to this, because people just live on their own and this isn't going on."[39]

He described the change that God has worked in his life in very non-theological but very vivid terms. He said it's as if "someone put his hand on me and turned me around and said, 'You're going the wrong way, stupid.'"

STORY FIVE

Glenelg Centre Baptist Church is located in a rural setting a few kilometres from the town of Durham, Ontario. This is the most rural of the churches that took part in the study. The area around the church is mostly open fields. The church is part of the Canadian Baptists of Ontario and Quebec. Glenelg can trace its origins back to meetings held in members' homes as far back as 1860.

Today the church averages between eighty and one hundred people in Sunday morning attendance. The demographic of the congregation includes larger families, a few singles, plenty of children, and mostly people who have been raised in Christian homes. The leaders of the church would describe it as being very conservative in both its theology and ecclesiology. They place a high value on membership, with more than 80 percent of the adults who attend the church accepted as members, who have an active role in the church.

The interview was with a young adult who has just graduated from high school. He's part of one of the leadership families at the church and as such has spent his whole life at Glenelg. He went through a period of rebellion when he was in high school; he didn't totally reject the gospel but questioned whether it had any relevance to his life. One of the problems he faced then was a lack of friends. He was the only male in the church youth group and did not relate well to the females. One of the major influences on his life at that time was music.

In grade eleven, at the invitation of a friend, he began to attend a different youth group, where he met other young men and established friendships. One of them introduced him to Christian hip-hop music. He began to question the moral value of the secular music he was listening to, and he asked God to give him a sign if he was to stop. At that time he had about one thousand songs on his computer, and only a small number were by Christian artists. One day, he saw that all of the secular songs had been wiped off his computer, but the Christian songs were still there. This was instrumental in bringing him to a point at which he recommitted his life to Christ.

While this experience was the key event in his spiritual journey back to Christ, relationships also played an important part. The first were with his parents. Throughout all of this period of searching he was constantly bringing his questions to his father. The other relationships were with his friends from the youth group. They were able to come around him and support him when he was in need of Christian friendship. He had many friends at school who were not Christians but none who could fill the spiritual needs in his life.

STORY SIX

The New Dundee Baptist Church is associated with the Canadian Baptists of Ontario and Quebec. The church was founded in 1852. Originally it was one of five preaching centres in Wilmot Township near the city of Kitchener. In the early years it was a German-speaking congregation, but in 1911 it became an English-speaking church. The town of New Dundee has about one thousand residents. The current pastor graduated from McMaster Divinity College, having majored in small-congregational studies. He is committed to working with small churches throughout his pastoral career.

The interview at New Dundee was with a single woman. She had gone through a difficult period in her life, having just come out of a broken relationship. During that time she lived right across the road from the pastor of the New Dundee church. The pastor and his wife would often meet her while on walks. Both owned dogs, which gave them something in common. Over time they became friends.

One day she decided that she "didn't have relationships with people that are great, so why not try God." As a result she knocked on the pastor's door and asked if she could go to church with his family. They responded that they would be delighted.

From the very first Sunday she felt accepted and welcomed at the church. She expressed it this way:

> "I always felt very welcome here, and it feels like they're my second family. They always love me, and even when I'm not here it's "Oh, where is she? We miss her." Wow, they actually care that much about me! It was almost a weird feeling, because I wasn't used to it. I mean, I have loved ones and friends and family, but it's just not the same feeling. So that's pretty much how it started."[40]

A relationship that began as two people walked their dogs in the morning resulted in a life transformation brought about through the work of the Holy Spirit in her life.

Summary

It's easy to feel like nothing's really happening in small-church settings, to be overwhelmed by the stories of mega-church successes. It's easy to feel like there's little the small church can do to impact the world. In my interviews there were no amazing stories of multiple conversions and major community impact. If such stories had existed, in all probability the church would no longer be small and would not qualify for the study. There were, however, seven people whose lives were transformed because of the impact of six small churches.

A young couple whose lives were falling apart found a spiritual family and new life in Christ at Pinewoods Gospel Church in Angus. A woman who had just gone through a time of intense stress following the birth of her child found support and new hope at Elmvale Community Church. Although he was not interviewed, her husband also came to faith in Christ through the witness of that church. A young woman from China became a Christian and is growing in her newfound faith as a result of the love and care of Bridletowne Park Church in Toronto. Her husband also became a Christian, and they are now raising their young child in a Christian community. A young man in his mid-thirties found an answer to his addictions to alcohol and drugs through the ministry of The Rock Community Church in Woodstock. His partner also has put her faith in Jesus Christ. A teenager was brought to a point of personal commitment to Christ through the impact of two small churches, Glenelg Centre Baptist Church and another church in whose youth group he found acceptance. Finally, a woman who had just come out of a bad relationship found what it meant to have a relationship with God through faith in Jesus Christ as a result of the impact of New Dundee Baptist Church on her life. They may not be the spectacular stories that are picked up by the Christian media, but in the lives of one or two people at a time, small churches are making a difference.

STEP FOUR
Carefully Rethink Your Mission

SIX

The Mission of God

A young woman recently asked me the following:

"What is the purpose of a Christian's life? A person puts her faith in Jesus and as a result has the promise of eternal life. Is the purpose for a person's life just that she will become a Christian so that she can go to heaven? Isn't there something in this life that should bring meaning to the Christian's life here on earth?"

That's a very insightful and important question. What is it that gives purpose to the Christian life? What is it that makes getting up every day an adventure rather than just the same old thing? To put it into very practical terms, why doesn't God just take every Christian to heaven the moment that that person becomes a Christian? If we become Christians in order to ensure ourselves a place in heaven, why doesn't God take us there immediately upon our conversion instead of allowing us to go through all of the problems and difficulties that are a part of this world?

The answer, both for the individual Christian and the church, lies in what Christopher J. H. Wright has called "The Mission of God."[41] While this chapter applies to the individual Christian, my focus will be discovering the purpose that God has for the church. To do that, it must be set in the context of the whole of Scripture and of God's ultimate mission. Notice that it's God's mission that we are searching for and not the church's mission.

The Bible begins with the story of creation. One thing is clear from the first two chapters of Genesis: God and God alone is responsible for the world's existence. To understand the author's purpose in telling the creation story, we must place it in the context in which it was written. With the exception of the Jewish nation, everyone worshipped a myriad of gods. They had a god for every purpose and part of life. A god of war was to bring victory in their many battles with neighbouring countries. A fertility god was to ensure that their crops would grow and that they would replenish the earth with children. There might even be a household god whose primary concern was for that one family that possessed it. Each group of people had their set of gods, and much of the conflict that occurred was seen as a battle of the gods. Whichever country emerged victorious obviously had the stronger gods.

The creation story presents us with a very different scenario, one that would have been radically different for everyone outside of the Jewish culture. The first two chapters of the Bible present the fact that this whole world came into existence by the work of one God. He was the Creator of everything that exists. There wasn't a pantheon of gods as the rest of the world believed, but one sovereign, all-powerful God who was Lord over everything. The remainder of the Old Testament is the playing out of this tension between the one true God on the one hand and the multitude of false gods on the other. These opening chapters establish the fact that the one God created the world in which we live. Everything else flows out of that fact.

As recorded in Genesis 3, the human race fell when Adam and Eve sinned. In Genesis 3–11, the author records in stark detail the impact of sin on the world. The murder of Abel (ch. 3), the destruction of the world by a flood (chs. 6–9), and the human pride behind the Tower of Babel (ch. 11) all demonstrate the universal fact of sin and the destructiveness that sin brings. The remainder of the Bible is the account of God's response to sin in the world.

Genesis 12 expresses a tension that is essential to understanding the unfolding story of the Bible. God is the Creator of the whole earth. He is the one true God, the God of all people. But, beginning with the twelfth chapter, God becomes uniquely the God of Israel. In reading the Bible one must always keep this tension between God as the universal God and God as uniquely the God of Israel. The focus of the Old Testament is largely on God as the God of the Jews, his chosen nation with whom he has entered into a covenant relationship. Always though there is the fact that he is the Creator of everything and as such the universal God who rules over everything. He is no tribal God as the false gods were.

The call of Abraham in Genesis 12:1–3 contains this tension. In that call, God sets in motion the events that will lead to Israel becoming God's unique people. There is, however, also a universal side to this passage that causes some commentators to refer to this as the Great Commission of the Old Testament. In this call, God makes it very clear that his purpose is not merely to establish a nation that will be in a special relationship with him but also to impact all people through this one special nation.

A detailed study of this passage would involve more room than this chapter allows, but two points are important to note. The first is that the central theme of this passage is blessing. In either noun or verb form the word *blessing* occurs five times in these three verses. God is going to *bless* Abram (v.2). God is going to be *a blessing* to others (v. 2). Those who *bless* Abram will be *blessed* (v. 3). But there can be no doubt that these blessings climax in the final phrase of verse 3: "*all peoples on earth will be* **blessed** *through you.*"

This brings us to the second point. There is a universal aspect to the blessing that God is going to bring. This blessing is not realized in its fullness until all the people on earth have been affected. The scope of the blessing far surpasses God's desire to bless Abram. God's purpose is to bring blessing to the whole world. He is going to do so through the nation that he has promised to Abram, but the scope of the blessing far exceeds that nation. Walter Kaiser captures the importance of this passage:

> It is our hope that the formative theology of Genesis 12:3 may once again be seen for what it is and has always been in the discussion of mission: a divine program to glorify himself by bringing salvation to all on planet Earth. Indeed, here is where

mission really begins. Here is the first Great Commission mandate of the Bible. It is this thesis that dominates the strategy, theology, and mission of the Old Testament.[42]

Any understanding of the purpose of the church must be placed in the context of these three foundational truths from the early chapters of Genesis. First, there is one God, who is the Creator of the universe and who is sovereign over all the earth. The story of the Jewish people throughout the Old Testament is the story of their constant battle to accept or reject this truth. On the one hand, they faced the ever-present temptation to worship the gods of the other nations around them. On the other hand, they were constantly being called back to covenant loyalty to the one true God who called Abram and promised to bless the world through Him. Since there is one sovereign God and the church is in covenant relationship with that God, the church's mission must be the mission of God.

Second, sin is a reality in the world, a reality that touches every single person and powerfully impacts society. The story of the Old Testament is the story of the impact of that sin and the incredible damage that it has done.

Over the past few years I've visited the country of Rwanda several times. In the capital city of Kigali the people of Rwanda have built a memorial to the genocide that took place there in 1994 in which almost one million people were killed in the space of just a few months. The memorial is part of their commitment to never forget the terror of that period. On more than one occasion, I've walked through that memorial. It's a gut-wrenching experience to view the reminders of the atrocities that were committed in those few months of murder. One can not observe the displays there without being deeply affected by the reality of sin. On the second floor of the memorial, visitors are taken through a history of genocide in the twentieth century. There are pictures and write-ups on the genocides in Bosnia, Cambodia, and other locations around the world. In the middle of the display is a reminder of the greatest genocide of the century, the Holocaust in Germany.

As I stood in that room looking at the horror that was portrayed, I was struck by the awfulness of sin as never before in my life. Millions of people from every part of the world lost their lives because sin with all of its horror is a reality of our lives here on this earth. It all began with that first act of disobedience in the Garden of Eden.

Finally, God has a plan for dealing with the impact of sin. His plan involves the creation of a special people, but their purpose is to bring blessing to the whole world. Christopher Wright points out that these two themes—universal sinfulness and God's mission to bring blessing—run parallel to each other throughout the entire Bible:

> When we combine the dark picture of Genesis 3–11 with the promise of blessing in chapter 12, we can anticipate that the story to follow will involve both realities. We know that we will be watching two scenarios unfolding together—just as Jesus said in his parable of the wheat and the weeds growing in the same field. On the one hand, we know that history will be the arena of human sin getting even worse. But on the other hand, we will now be watching for the footprints of God's blessing for all nations through the nation to emerge from the loins of Abraham. Blessing will take on a historical dimension injecting hope and faith into an otherwise dark and depressing narrative.[43]

In the New Testament, in the person and work of Jesus, this promise made to Abraham centuries before is fulfilled. Jesus is God's answer to sin. In Jesus' death and resurrection, God dealt with the issue of sin once and for all. Jesus himself pointed this out to his disciples after his resurrection. In Luke 24:44, Jesus stated that all of the Old Testament Scriptures pointed to this. He encompasses all of the Old Testament by including the major divisions in the Jewish Scriptures—the Law, the Prophets, and the Psalms.

In Luke 24:46–47, Luke lists the events to which the Old Testament Scriptures point. First, *"the Christ will suffer."* Second, He will *"rise from the dead on the third day."* Third, *"repentance and forgiveness of sins will be preached in his name to all nations, beginning at Jerusalem.*" The first two are the heart of the gospel. The third is essential if the blessing is going to extend beyond the narrow geographical and cultural confines in which Jesus lived his life here on earth.

The Old Testament Scriptures point to the fact that mission is at the heart of God's purpose for his world. It's not enough just to read the Old Testament with a Christological understanding. When a church or an individual becomes involved in the mission of taking the news about Jesus Christ to the world, whether that is to another country or to the person next door, that individual becomes part of fulfilling the mission of God. He or she becomes part of extending the blessing talked about in Genesis 12:3 to all peoples. Our understanding of the church's purpose must be grounded in an understanding of God's desire to bless the whole world. Wright puts this all into a proper perspective:

> It is not so much the case that God has a mission for his church in the world, as that God has a church for his mission in the world. Mission was not made for the church; the church was made for mission—God's mission.[44]

Church leaders have invested long hours into defining a vision statement for their church. There can be value in this, but before doing so it is essential to realize that the challenge is not to define the church's mission but to discover God's mission and become a part of it. God does have a mission, and the purpose of that mission is to be a blessing to the whole world.

This chapter began with a question and will close with the answer. Whether we are talking about individual purpose or purpose that includes the whole church, meaning in life comes out of understanding that God has a mission that is far bigger than anything that we might envision, and he is calling us to be part of bringing that mission to completion.

Far too often people in our churches don't see anything beyond the immediate task in which they are involved. The Sunday school teacher is painfully aware of the hours spent in preparing to teach a class of children. The youth leaders know that they give up valuable evenings, often on weekends, in order to spend time with someone else's teenagers. The leadership team spends hours working through what might seem like trivial issues, often arriving home late when they have to get up early the next morning for another day at work. Even pastors can get caught up in the endless hours of study time that must go into a sermon that once preached can never be preached again. It's possible to see only the time and effort involved in service and miss out on the blessing that comes from being part of God's mission in this world.

Sunday school teachers are helping to build a foundation in children's lives upon which their whole future walk with God will be built. They are contributing to the Christian values that will become the cornerstone of these children's lives in years to come. Youth leaders are investing into the lives of future leaders at possibly the most crucial time that they will ever go through. The sacrificial hours the leaders give will contribute towards those young people capturing the vision for future service that they in turn will invest into the lives of other people. As I look back over my own life at the people who invested in me and made a significant contribution to my growth, the couple who led our youth group when I was in high school are right at the top of that list. Not only did they sacrifice their time but they challenged me to become all that God wants me to be.

Whatever the area of service in which we are involved, we need to see beyond the immediate demands of the job and see ourselves as part of what God is doing as he carries out his mission. It's only when we do this that we can experience the thrill of being used by God to accomplish his purpose for our world.

Many churches have a vision statement written on paper and put on a shelf, never to make a serious difference in the life of the church. Every church needs to have the clear understanding, written not on paper but on people's hearts, that God has a mission and that he wants each and every Christian to be part of that mission. When that happens, churches will come alive with the realization that the Christian life really does have purpose and meaning and that every day is an adventure worth living.

SEVEN

The Kingdom of God

One of my memories is listening as a child to some adults debate whether the Kingdom of Heaven and the Kingdom of God refer to the same thing. I grew up in a home in which dispensational theology was the undisputed king, and to hold to anything else was tantamount to heresy. When I was still in high school and dating the young woman who became my wife, I decided to give her a new Bible as a gift on her eighteenth birthday. I talked it over with my pastor and was assured that if I wanted to give her the best, there was nothing better than the Scofield Study Bible. It was solidly King James and full of study notes that would keep her on the right track for as long as she used them.

A long time ago she stopped using the King James and stopped reading the study notes, and she has moved a long way from the "dispensational orthodoxy" of her youth. She still has that Bible, but I like to think that it's the sentimental attachment as a gift from me that keeps it on her shelf.

What bothers me is that the adults who were debating the relationship between the Kingdom of God and the Kingdom of Heaven were more concerned about getting their definitions right than about living out the values of the Kingdom here on this earth. I'm not going to answer all of the theological questions concerning the Kingdom, but I will look at the central place that it should hold for anyone who's serious about finding God's mission for the church.

One of my favourite quotes out of all the reading that I've done over my lifetime comes from John Stott's writings:

Christianity is Christ. The persona and work of Christ are the rock upon which the Christian religion is built. If he is not who he said he was, and if he did not do what he said he had come to do, the foundation is undermined and the whole superstructure will collapse. Take Christ from Christianity and you disembowel it; there is practically nothing left. Christ is the centre of Christianity; all else is circumference.[45]

If Stott is right about the centrality of Jesus in the Christian faith—and almost all biblical scholars would agree with him—then every component of our faith must be defined by the life, death and resurrection of Jesus. Everything that Christians do must be determined by the teaching and ministry of Jesus when he was here on earth. If believers are to do this, they need to understand the central message of Jesus and then build their lives as Christians around that central message.

The central core of Jesus' message was the Kingdom of God. This can be seen throughout the life and ministry of Jesus. Mark summarized the preaching of Jesus as a call to repentance because the Kingdom of God is near (Mark 1:15). Jesus described his ministry as preaching *"the good news of the kingdom of God"* (Luke 4:43). Many of the parables that he taught were about the Kingdom (Matthew 13:11, 24, 31, 44, 47). The power encounters that Jesus had with the demonic world are described in Kingdom terms (Matthew 12:25–28). People are exhorted to seek God's Kingdom (Matthew 5:33). Jesus talked about the requirements and the challenges of entry into the Kingdom (Matthew 18:3; 19:23–24). He talked about the necessity of the new birth if one was going to see the Kingdom (John 3:3). The subject of the Kingdom was the focus of his post-resurrection teaching (Acts 1:3). These are but a few examples of what was the core of Jesus' whole ministry. His message was a message about the Kingdom because in his person the Kingdom of God had come into the world in a totally unique way. As George Eldon Ladd points out, "This was not a new theology or new idea or new promise; it was a new event in history."[46] In the person of Jesus, God's Kingdom had come.

It's important to note that the Kingdom is God's. It's not just another kingdom in a long list of earthly kingdoms. This is God's Kingdom. This adds an important note of seriousness for every congregation as they attempt to understand what it means to work as part of the Kingdom. The decisions made by church leaders need to reflect the leading and the character of God. There is no more important role for church leaders than to discern the leading of God in the issues they face. They are part of his Kingdom, and the decisions they make need to reflect that fact.

One of the tensions in Christian living is that the Kingdom is both present and future. This captures an essential biblical truth. If we see the Kingdom as only a theological truth that will find fulfillment at some point in the future, it will have little impact on our lives in the present. It needs to be much more than that. It needs to be the dynamic power that is at work in the social and political structures of this world and in the lives of individuals who are committed to following Jesus Christ as his disciples.

The Kingdom of God is central to the teaching and ministry of Jesus. It is dynamically active in the lives of God's people, both individually and collectively in the church today. As such it needs to be at the heart of everything we do within the church. One of those areas is evangelism. William Abraham brings a much needed emphasis to this point:

> Any considered attempt to develop a coherent concept of evangelism that will be serviceable in the present must begin with eschatology. Whatever evangelism may be, it is at least ultimately related to the gospel of the reign of God that was inaugurated in the life, death and resurrection of Jesus of Nazareth. Any vision of evangelism that ignores the kingdom of God, or relegates it to a position of secondary importance, or fails to wrestle thoroughly with its content is destined at the outset to fail. This is so because the kingdom of God is absolutely central to the ministry of Jesus and to the mission of the disciples that launched the Christian movement into history.[47]

Rodney Clapp suggests that "evangelism needs to be understood not simply as declaring a message to someone but as an initiation into the world-changing kingdom of God."[48] In evangelism we are inviting people not only to make a decision for Christ but to become part of the Kingdom of God. Evangelism needs to be wrapped up in everything the church does, because everything the church does is part of what it means to be part of the Kingdom of God. Too often evangelism has been separated from the church and entrusted to individuals or para-church organizations. In too many cases churches have been reluctant to become involved in evangelism. Behind this lies a very narrow view of what constitutes evangelism. It is seen as one activity of the church rather than something that is integrated into every facet of church life.

When we see evangelism as an invitation extended to people to become part of this Kingdom, which was inaugurated by Jesus and continues today as a dynamic force played out in the church through his followers, it broadens our understanding of what evangelism involves. Rather than simply inviting people to make a decision for Christ, we are inviting them into a whole new way of living that is defined by the reign of God over their lives.

For a long time, the relationship between evangelism and social action has been the subject of theological debate. If the life and ministry of Jesus is our guiding principle, it's hard to understand how this tension ever developed in the first place. One cannot read the Gospels without being struck by the fact that Jesus was deeply involved in both evangelism and social action. He spent a significant amount of his time teaching his followers what it meant to be part of God's Kingdom. Verbal proclamation was an important part of his ministry.

He also spent considerable time meeting the needs of people. He healed the sick, raised the dead, restored sight to the blind, and fed the hungry. Significant in all of this is the natural way he integrated the two. This may be no more evident than in his quotation from Isaiah 61 when he preached in the synagogue at Nazareth (Luke 4:14–19). The passage he quoted contains a proclamation of good news, the healing of physical needs, and concern for the oppressed. All of these were a natural part of Jesus' ministry, and all need to be part of the church's ministry as we act as God's agents, entrusted with the responsibility of making the Kingdom visible in our world today.

In 1974 the first International Congress on World Evangelization was held in Lausanne, Switzerland, with more than 2,300 people from 150 countries in attendance. Two significant developments came out of that initial congress. The Lausanne Continuation Committee, which became the Lausanne Committee for World Evangelization in 1976, was established to continue to move towards the fulfillment of the goals of the congress. Secondly, the Lausanne Covenant was drawn up and signed by those attending the congress.

In 1989 a second congress was held in Manila, Philippines, with 4,300 people from 173 countries in attendance. This congress produced the Manila Manifesto.

In 2010 a third congress was held in Cape Town, South Africa, with more than 4,000 people from 198 countries attending. Modern technology enabled thousands more around the world to participate. This congress produced the Cape Town Commitment.

In addition to these three large congresses, the Lausanne Committee has held numerous smaller meetings that have produced occasional papers on a number of different topics. One of those topics was the relationship between evangelism and social action. In the very first congress in Lausanne, Billy Graham stated this as one of the goals. One of the most important accomplishments of the congress was that the Lausanne Covenant contained a very clear statement concerning this relationship. While emphasizing the importance of both evangelism and social responsibility, the covenant stated that evangelism was primary. The covenant did not expand on exactly what that meant.

In 1982, a group of fifty leaders from twenty-seven different countries met in Grand Rapids, Michigan, to discuss this issue. They produced a report in which they expanded on the relationship between the two, linking them together as being indispensable to each other. They still endorsed the primacy of evangelism but stated that the choice between the two is largely conceptual. In practical terms, the two are both an indispensable part of the responsibility of the Christian. The Manila Manifesto endorsed this position.

The Cape Town Commitment reiterates the relationship between evangelism and social responsibility but without acknowledging the primacy of evangelism. It treats the two as parts of the same task. The commitment goes to great length to define exactly what it means to live out our social responsibility in many different areas, such as pluralism, emerging technologies, slavery and human trafficking, to name just a few. Being part of the Kingdom of God has very practical implications.

The discussion concerning the relationship between evangelism and social responsibility has been an important one. The temptation is to err on one side or the other. For many years in evangelical churches, people have erred on the side of evangelism only. Concern for social responsibility was seen as an indication that someone was becoming liberal in his or her theology. This is sad in that at one time Christians were at the forefront of much of the social change that took place. William Wilberforce fought against slavery and was largely instrumental in seeing it abolished in the British Empire. Elizabeth Fry led the movement that resulted in major prison reform in England. George Muller provided care for thousands of orphans in Bristol. These are just three of many examples of evangelical leaders who saw clearly their responsibility to fight against social evils and as a result changed the culture in which they lived. They believed that being a Christian involved much more than just sharing a verbal message that could result in the transformation of individual lives. They also saw their Christian responsibility as including a battle against the social evils they faced in their day.

On the other hand, there's a danger that as the church rediscovers its biblical mandate to be involved in meeting the social needs of society, the verbal witness to the gospel could be lost. It's true that Jesus spent much of his time meeting the social needs of people, but he also spent time teaching them about the Kingdom of God and the need to be born again into that Kingdom. In the book of Acts, his disciples continued this balanced ministry. Luke gives us examples of evangelistic sermons and the response of people to that verbal sharing of the gospel. At the same time, he gives us examples of how they responded to people's physical needs through healing the sick and providing for the poor.

For much of its history the Lausanne Movement has talked about the primacy of evangelism over social responsibility. This has been an awkward distinction, by their own admission. While they have given evangelism the priority, they have recognized that this is more of a theoretical distinction than a practical one. In the working out of these two responsibilities, the movement has recognized that they are inseparable partners. Christopher Wright has described the relationship between the two as a relationship of "ultimacy" rather than one of "primacy," which I believe provides a much better distinction:

> This is why I speak of ultimacy rather than primacy. Mission may not always begin with evangelism. But mission that does not ultimately include the Word and the name of Christ, the call of repentance, and faith and obedience has not completed its task. It is defective mission, not holistic mission.[49]

The key to this whole debate is to remember that it's much more than just a theological debate. There are hurting people in our communities who need to both hear the message of the gospel and have loving people respond to their needs. When both of these elements are practiced by the church, something very powerful is unleashed.

The Kingdom of God is not a hoped-for possibility but a present reality. This is the church's incentive to be involved in evangelism and social action. As believers we are part of God's Kingdom, and we have the privilege of inviting others to come and join us in the blessings and responsibilities that membership entails. When we do that, we are continuing the work of Jesus and playing our part in the mission that God has in this world.

EIGHT

The Danger of Defining Conversion Too Narrowly

At one point in my pastoral experience, I was helping out with a junior high youth group. We were having serious problems with two of the boys. They would not behave, causing problems not only for the leaders but for the rest of the children as well. Finally we called a meeting of the leaders to discuss what we should do, since we couldn't just let things continue. The discussion finally came around to whether we should just expel the two from the group, thus removing the problem completely.

One of the leaders expressed her reservations about taking that step. One of the boys had made a profession of faith in a different context about one year earlier, but the other boy had never taken that step. The problem for her was that the second boy would go to hell if he died. Regardless of how many problems he caused, we had to keep him in an environment in which he might be led to pray the prayer so that his eternal security would be set. I didn't say anything at the time, but I have thought about that conversation many times since. That leader was trying to reach out to these children in all sincerity but doing so with a very flawed theological understanding of what conversion is.

A clear understanding of conversion is absolutely essential to evangelism and ultimately to every aspect of church life. Without such an understanding people are on a journey through dense bush without a compass. They may be making excellent time, but without some knowledge of where they're going, they'll probably arrive at the wrong destination. Too often people are pressured into making decisions without any clear understanding of their destination. The result is that most churches have more spiritual abortions than live births in their pursuit to see people born again into the Kingdom of God. Many evangelical churches place a strong emphasis on children's ministry with the intent of getting children to profess faith in Jesus Christ, believing that if they do this, the children will be assured of going to heaven. They work with these children when they're young, but when they become teenagers the children disappear from the clubs, Sunday schools and junior youth groups, never to be seen again. Leaders console themselves with the idea that at least they prayed a prayer at some point along the way and thus bought themselves a ticket to heaven.

This thinking has several serious flaws in it. The first is that it gives churches a false assurance that they are carrying out successful evangelism when in reality they are accomplishing very little of any eternal significance. The second problem is that they may be giving children a false sense of spiritual security when there is no theological foundation on which to build their hope. Finally, such an approach allows churches to ignore the call to produce disciples, which involves a much greater investment into the lives of children than many churches are willing to make. This has practical implications as to how we do evangelism and, in this case, how we work with children and teenagers.

Scholars disagree on the number and nature of the elements that go into a genuine conversion. Richard Peace suggests three elements: insight, turning, and transformation.[50] Paul Helm also lists three elements: saving faith, conviction of sin, and true repentance.[51] Gordon T. Smith lists seven elements: belief in Jesus, repentance, trust in Christ Jesus, transfer of allegiance, baptism, reception of the gift of the Holy Spirit, and incorporation into congregational life.[52] While these scholars may not agree on the number and nature of the elements, they are in total agreement that conversion is more than a simple decision with few implications for life thereafter. Conversion is much more than simply praying a prayer and having the assurance of eternal life.

Like Peace and Helm I'm going to limit myself to three elements, all of which are essential in the conversion experience. The Bible makes it very clear that for conversion to happen, there must be faith. For conversion to happen, there must also be turning. Finally, for conversion to happen there must be transformation. I am indebted to Richard Peace for the last two of these terms.

Faith

Paul is very clear that the essential element in conversion is faith (Romans 1:16–17; Galatians 3:11; Ephesians 2:8–9). For faith to be meaningful there must be belief in something concrete. There must be a clear understanding of the content of the gospel if conversion is going to take place. Otherwise, faith is meaningless. The person must have an understanding of who Jesus is and what he has done. The person must have an understanding of sin and its impact on the world and on the individual. There must be some understanding of the sacrificial nature of Christ's death on the cross. Finally, there must be some understanding of the implications involved in taking a step of faith and becoming a follower of Jesus Christ. I realize that there can be serious debate over the inclusion of the four elements that I have listed here and the exclusion of others, but the point is that there must be content. A person must have something in which to believe if he is going to exercise faith.

Too often people are presented with a canned approach to evangelism and then asked to accept Jesus into their lives without any understanding of the full scope of the gospel message. People cannot respond in faith without a clear understanding of what they are being asked to believe. Recognizing that there is a huge theological question surrounding the part God plays and the part people play in this saving faith, it's clear that whatever the origin of that faith, there must be content for it to be effective.

It's at this point that many Christians have a faulty understanding of evangelism. When the focus is on decisions, too often the challenge is to get someone to pray a prayer. This prayer then becomes the indication that a decision has been made. In too many evangelical churches, the sinner's prayer has become the key ingredient in the conversion process. Churches have substituted a prayer for faith. They can clearly know when a prayer has been prayed, and that allows them to keep their statistics by which they measure the success or failure of their evangelistic endeavours.

Humans cannot measure faith. Faith is something that is inward, something that only God knows for sure whether it is truly there. When people try to determine the genuineness of someone's conversion they are trying to put themselves in the place of God. Their responsibility is to share the content of the gospel in a faithful and persuasive way under the direction of the Holy Spirit.

Years ago many churches held two services on Sundays. There was a service in the morning designed primarily for Christians, with an emphasis on worship and instruction for the members. In the evening a second service was held. Often this service was evangelistic in nature, with a gospel message focused primarily on Jesus and his death on the cross. Over the years, attendance at evening services dwindled to the point at which church after church stopped holding any kind of Sunday evening service. That has probably been a necessary part of the evolution of the Christian church in Canada.

We live in a very different cultural backdrop from what people experienced fifty years ago. I'm not calling for a reinstatement of an evening service. There was, however, something lost when churches dropped that service. For all its faults—and there were many—the Sunday evening service provided a setting in which the content of the gospel was shared. Often there weren't any unchurched people at those services, but they still provided that avenue for the gospel to be preached. Unfortunately, most churches have not provided another setting for this to happen in. There isn't a setting to which people can bring others to hear the content of the gospel so that when they are challenged to respond they know what they're responding to.

Turning

The second essential element in conversion is the action of turning. Peace describes what is involved in this:

> So there was a turning on Paul's part—from the law to Christ, from persecution to apostleship, from killing Jews who had become Christians to calling Gentiles to become Christians. This is what lies at the heart of the word "conversion"—the

image of turning. There are a *from* and a *to*. The old is renounced (turning from) and the new is embraced (turning to).[53]

Without turning there is no conversion. The idea that someone can claim to have experienced conversion and continue on as if nothing had changed is contrary to the very meaning of the word. Something *must* change. This turning is often at the heart of the conversion stories that everyone likes to hear. God comes into a life and totally changes that person into something completely new. As Peace has pointed out, the apostle Paul is perhaps the most radical example of this kind of change in the New Testament.

An important element in this turning is repentance. There must be a recognition of sin and an understanding of the need for forgiveness if someone is going to turn from a life controlled by sin to a life controlled by the Holy Spirit. Paul describes this as moving from being "*slaves to sin*" to being "*slaves to righteousness*" (Romans 6:15–18). This is what repentance is all about, a willingness to turn.

Transformation

The final element in conversion is transformation. Paul describes the transformation that takes place as becoming an entirely new creation (2 Corinthians 5:17). Jesus describes it as a new birth (John 3:3). Paul also describes it as being given new life when we are dead to sin (Ephesians 2:4–5). These are but three of the many ways in which the New Testament describes the transformation that takes place when a person experiences true conversion. The thing that is absolutely clear, whatever picture is used, is that when a person experiences conversion a drastic change takes place, and that change must be reflected in the person's life.

Perhaps the most extensive teaching on this is found in Jesus' words in the fifteenth chapter of John. Jesus is talking about the fact that if a person abides in him, that person will bear fruit. If he doesn't abide in Jesus, he will not bear fruit, and the gardener will prune the branch and remove it from its place in the vine. It's important to note that a branch is not part of the vine because it bears fruit. The branch bears fruit because it is part of the vine (v. 5). The natural result of being part of the vine is that the branch bears fruit. A person is not in relationship with Jesus Christ and thus a Christian because he bears fruit. Rather, he bears fruit because he is in relationship with Jesus Christ and thus a Christian, and the natural result of that relationship is to bear fruit. If there is no fruit, it's questionable if the person is in relationship with Christ. A person cannot be an adopted child of God, born again into relationship with God, forgiven, justified, indwelt by the Holy Spirit, in fellowship with the rest of God's family, dead to sin and alive to Jesus Christ, without it making an obvious difference in that person's life. Transformation will happen when a person experiences true conversion, which unleashes all of the power of the Holy Spirit to bring about the changes that are meant to occur.

The question of transformation reflects the Great Commission's call to make disciples. It reflects the understanding of evangelism as inviting people to become part of God's Kingdom here on earth and to experience the dynamic power of that Kingdom in their lives. Ultimately it reflects the foundational truth that God has a plan for his world and his people that goes beyond just the experience of having their sins forgiven so that they can go to heaven. God's plan is that people will experience blessing through Jesus Christ; they will grow into the kind of disciples who go out to invite others into that Kingdom; they will become equipped to be part of all this as they experience the transformation that conversion brings into their lives.

One other aspect of conversion needs to be addressed. Any method of evangelism designed to produce cookie-cutter decisions needs to be rejected. Every person's conversion experience needs to be uniquely her own. I grew up in a setting in which conversion was measured by very narrow parameters. Those parameters were so narrow that the conversion of John Wesley was even called into question. His famous testimony of what he experienced on May 24, 1738, in the meeting at Aldersgate Street in London was not tied to a specific verse of Scripture and was therefore questionable. In that church the belief was that for a conversion to be genuine there had to be a verse of Scripture that God used to convict the person and draw that person to Christ. Any understanding of conversion must be broad enough to accommodate a wide variety of experiences.

There has been debate over whether conversion comes about as the result of a simple, definite, one-time crisis experience, such as the apostle Paul experienced, or through a process over time, such as may have been experienced by the twelve disciples. In actual fact, God uses many different means of bringing people to that decisive moment of faith. It may be a crisis experience, but it may also be the result of a slow process during which multiple people contribute to the journey into faith. God is not restricted to only one method in working in people's lives. Rather, he works according to the unique circumstances, personality, and history of each person as he brings them to faith. As people through whom God wishes to work, we need to be as open as he is in the ways in which we share our faith. However he chooses to work, we need to celebrate that someone has come into relationship with God and that God gave us the incredible privilege of being part of the process.

STEP FIVE
Expectantly Shape Your Vision

NINE

The Importance of Vision

In my early days as a pastor, in the church from which I was fired, I decided to involve the leadership team there in setting a vision for the church. I asked each of them to share what they thought was the main priority in the ministry.

With little hesitation the first said that the priority in any church had to be preaching. If a church was going to grow, it needed solid, Bible-centred preaching. Whatever I did, I needed to make sure that I built into my schedule enough study time to produce the kind of quality sermons that would affect people.

The second elder reached back into the history of the church and shared that it had been started as a children's outreach ministry. A group of young adults from an inner city church had come into the area in order to run a Sunday school there on Sunday afternoons. The church had developed out of that work with children. Whatever we did, we had to protect that heritage. Work with children had to be a high priority.

The third elder also reached back into history but from a different perspective. He pointed out that twice before the church had lost almost all of its teenagers. They had faced two different crises with the youth, and in both cases the result had been a mass exodus of teenagers. Whatever else the church might do, we had to have a solid youth program, because we couldn't afford to lose the youth again. Those young people were the future of the church.

The fourth elder believed that evangelism had to be at the heart of what the church did. They had not been successful in reaching out to the community, and since this was the biblical imperative for any church, what was happening was not acceptable. There were people all around us who were going to hell, and we needed to take the message of salvation to them. We needed more evangelism in the church.

The fifth elder shared that, while all of these things were important, what really needed to be at the heart of church life was community. If we weren't developing community, then everything else was going to fail anyways. The people within the church had to care for each other first, and then they could reach out to others.

I remember leaving that meeting with a deep sense of hopelessness. I felt a little like a drowning man who had just been thrown a concrete block instead of a life preserver. All that I had to do to please the elders was study forty hours a week so that I prepared dynamic, life-changing sermons, lead a thriving children's program, pour untold hours into the youth, develop an outstanding small group ministry so that everyone in the church felt wanted, and in my spare time reach the entire neighbourhood for Christ. That's a little bit of an exaggeration, but it's how I felt at the end of the meeting.

Life would have been so much easier if those elders had just had foolish ideas of what the church should be and where it should go. Then I could have dismissed everything they said and got on with the task of leading the church. The problem was that much of what they shared was dead on. Those things *were* important. I could not simply dismiss them as being irrelevant. But each elder had a different vision for the church. It left me as the pastor feeling like I was tied to five horses, each of which was pulling in a different direction. It was only going to be a matter of time before I was pulled to pieces.

Vision and purpose are important in any church but only when they are shared vision and purpose. Everything that Jesus did, He did out of a sense of purpose. From childhood to His ascension back to heaven everything was done with a clear reason for his actions. As a twelve-year-old boy he told his frantic parents that he was in the temple for a purpose. *"Why were you searching for me?...Didn't you know I had to be in my Father's house?"* (Luke 2:49).

After Peter's confession at Caesarea Philippi, Jesus outlined the future for his disciples.

> *From that time on Jesus began to explain to his disciples that he must go to Jerusalem and suffer many things at the hands of the elders, chief priests and teachers of the law, and that he must be killed and on the third day be raised to life.* (Matthew 16:21)

Just before his death as he met with the disciples in the upper room he described the purpose of His entire ministry. "*I have brought you glory on earth by completing the work you gave me to do. And now, Father, glorify me in your presence with the glory I had with you before the world began*" (John 17:4–5).

Many other passages could be quoted to illustrate the sense of purpose that governed all that Jesus did. Following his ascension, his followers began to spread the gospel with the same sense of purpose. Even when standing before the rulers in Jerusalem, knowing that their lives were on the line, the disciples were driven by that sense of purpose. "*But Peter and John replied, 'Judge for yourselves whether it is right in God's sight to obey you rather than God. For we cannot help speaking about what we have seen and heard'*" (Acts 4:19–20).

At the point of Paul's conversion, Ananias was given a clear sense of Paul's purpose by God Himself. "*This man is my chosen instrument to carry my name before the Gentiles and their kings and before the people of Israel. I will show him how much he must suffer for my name*" (Acts 9:15–16).

Yet reality is that most churches operate without any clear sense of purpose. They may be driven by a lot of different pressures, but they have never clearly spelled out their vision for their church and allowed that vision to be the motivating force behind what they are doing.

I remember reading a comic strip once in which a young boy shot an arrow. He then took some paint, went up to the arrow, which was sticking in the fence, and drew a target around it. It might have made him feel better in the immediate, but it probably didn't do anything to improve his accuracy as an archer. I think it was an all too accurate picture of what happens in many churches. We simply react to what happens, allowing circumstances to determine the direction we go in.

Many authors stress the difference between a vision statement and a mission statement. If a church is to take seriously the process of establishing a sense of purpose, the distinction between these two can be an important part of the process. For many churches, however, the distinction is more confusing than it is helpful. Church leaders can spend more time trying to figure out the difference than they spend actually implementing the vision. For that reason I am limiting myself to the one phrase—vision statement—and using it to refer to the whole process.

The Importance of Vision

If you want to know if you have the gift of leadership, look behind you. If there's no one there following you, you probably aren't a leader. On the other hand, those who are following want to know that their leader is actually taking them someplace. They want to follow someone with vision.

Almost every leadership book I've read at some point stressed the importance of vision. George Barna considered it so important that he wrote an entire book on it.

> Realize that the true ministry begins with vision. For a Christian leader—that is an individual chosen by God to move His people forward—vision is not to be regarded as an option. It is the insight that instructs the leader and directs his or her path. If for whatever reason, you are attempting to lead God's people without God's vision for your ministry, you are simply playing a dangerous game. It is a game that neither pleases God nor satisfies people.[54]

Aubrey Malphurs also stresses the need for vision:

> The leader of the ministry must have a clear vision, but so must the people in the church if it's to become a reality. It's vital that every believer in your church see and pursue both his or her own vision and the church's vision. This honors the Christian's own unique design and God's vision for his or her life, and it honors fellow believers at the local church level.[55]

I could go on quoting authors on this subject of vision until the book is filled up with nothing else, but I've made my point. People who write on the subject of leadership in the church stress the importance of vision.

While in my early twenties I spent two years serving as part of a church planting team in Barranquilla, Colombia. One of the advantages of that location was that we were only a few miles from the Caribbean. The disadvantage was the incredible heat and humidity that made an afternoon at the beach a welcome event.

One of those visits to the beach almost turned out to be the last thing I did here on earth. In the area where we swam, there were numerous sandbars. On this particular afternoon I decided to see how far I could swim out and still find sandbars on which to stand. I would swim a short distance, and sure enough, there would be another sandbar. Finally I reached the point at which there were no more sandbars. I had turned around to head back to shore when I realized that a current was pulling me back into the deeper water. I would swim for a while and try to touch bottom, but as soon as I stopped swimming I would be carried farther from shore.

After swimming for what seemed like a long time, I wasn't any closer to the shore than when I started, and I began to think that maybe I would never reach it. Finally I identified a landmark on the shore, put my head down, and just swam for that landmark for all I was worth. I refused to try to touch bottom until I was so close to shore that I knew I was safe. Without the sense of direction that the landmark gave me I would probably never have made it out of the ocean that day.

Many churches are being carried along by whatever currents come their way. They're being dragged this way and that way without any clear sense of where they need to go. They need to find a landmark that they can head towards, and, ignoring everything else, they need to move towards that mark. It's only clear vision that gives a church that sense of purpose.

The Futility of an Unused Vision Statement

A couple of years ago I was invited by a leadership team to advise them on a vision statement that they were in the process of putting together.

They had already spent a lot of time working on the wording, and they were almost satisfied with it. They just wanted some final confirmation. I met with them several times, during which we looked at the wording. It was obvious that they had put a lot of thought into it. It met most of the requirements for a good vision statement. It captured what they wanted to see happen in the church. It was worded in a way that anyone would be able to understand it. It was solidly biblical.

I could find very little wrong with what they had done. I did, however, give them a strong warning. They were ready to announce the statement to the church. The church had had almost no input into the statement, but there wasn't any strong opposition to it. My fear was that they would do what countless other churches had done before them. I was afraid that they would announce the statement and then never actually put it to use.

The leaders announced the vision. They even had it printed on the front page of their bulletin every Sunday. Unfortunately, in the three years that have passed since, not one decision has been affected by that vision statement. In fact, recently not one of the current elders could tell me without looking what the statement said.

Reality is that for many churches the task of developing a vision statement is an enormous waste of time. Leaders put hours into trying to make sure that the wording is just right. They try to capture the biblical direction for their church in a memorable statement. They share this statement with the church family. Then they put the statement on a shelf and never use it again. They might trot it out when someone asks about their church, but they don't allow the vision to affect any part of their church life. If a vision doesn't determine a church's direction, it really isn't a vision. It's just another exercise that takes time and energy away from more important things. If you have to blow the dust off your vision statement, it isn't really a vision statement. It's just a collection of words.

No one has advocated the importance of vision or purpose for a church more than Rick Warren over the past few decades. He makes the point that simply developing a vision statement isn't enough:

Now we come to the most difficult part of becoming a purpose-driven church. Many churches have done all I've talked about in the previous chapters: They have defined their purposes and developed a purpose statement; they regularly communicate their purposes to their membership; they have even reorganized their structure around their purposes. However, a purpose-driven church must go one step further and rigorously apply its purpose to every part of the church: programming, scheduling, budgeting, staffing, preaching and so forth.[56]

Warren has hit the nail right on the head. This is the most difficult part of developing a vision statement, but it is the indispensable part. Vision only truly becomes vision when it is applied to every part of church life. It's at this point that the majority of churches fail. They don't allow the vision to become the driving force in all that their church does. They don't evaluate current programs by their contribution to seeing the vision become reality. They don't determine future programs by how much those programs contribute to the vision. They don't plan their preaching schedule or place people in key leadership positions on the basis of the vision.

A very simple question to ask about any church's vision statement is: "In what way has this statement changed how we do church?" If the answer is that it hasn't changed it at all, whatever else those words on the paper might be, they don't define a vision for that church.

A Biblical Perspective

In defining reality in most churches we see that two things are true. The first is that vision is an important element of church health. The second is that most churches that invest the time and effort to develop a vision statement never actually use it in the practical outworking of their church life. So how do we develop a vision that is simple enough for every church to use in shaping its future direction?

Jesus gave us the answer to that question just before he ascended to heaven. It comes out of the Great Commission, Jesus' final directive to his disciples.

You may already have developed a vision statement for your church. If you have and you are actually using it to shape your future direction, I commend you. My guess is that it probably encompasses the Great Commission in some form. If it doesn't, then perhaps you need to rethink the statement, because whatever we create will not be better than what Jesus himself gave to his church. An effective statement will probably be written in language that is easily understood by people today, but it should contain the main focus of Christ's words found in Matthew 28:18–20.

The actual commission is bookended by two statements that establish a context for the commission itself. In verse 18 Jesus establishes the authority needed to put the commission into effect. Every Christian in every church needs to be reminded that she does not serve in her own authority. We are a sent people, and we are sent by the One who holds all authority in his hands. Every person who serves in government knows that there's a significant difference between giving a personal opinion on a subject and speaking on behalf of the government. If he has been designated as the government spokesperson, his words carry the weight of the entire country behind them.

Jesus has been given all authority. There are two interesting contrasts that can be drawn from this truth. First, there is the contrast between this statement and the death of Jesus. Just a few weeks before, he had seemed to be under the control of his captors. He stood silent before those who seemed to have the ultimate authority. The Jewish leaders took him captive and put him on trial. They beat him and tortured him. Finally they took him before Pilate, the ultimate voice of authority in Palestine at that time. Pilate represented Caesar, the final authority in Rome. With the consent of the Jewish leaders, the Roman governor pronounced sentence, and they took Jesus out and put him to death. What greater demonstration of their authority could they possibly have made? Yet just a few short weeks later the Risen Christ is telling his disciples that his authority is greater than all of these other rulers.

There's a continuum in the level of authority represented here. The authority of Pilate was greater than that of the Jewish leaders. The authority of Caesar was greater than Pilate's. But Jesus' authority is greater than all of them—Jewish leaders, the Roman governor, and even Caesar on the throne in Rome. All authority has been given to Jesus.

There is also an interesting contrast between this statement and the temptation of Jesus. In the second of the three tests, Satan offered to give to Jesus all the kingdoms of the earth, with the authority that went with them. If Jesus would just bow down and worship Satan, the world with its authority could be his (Luke 4:5–8). But Jesus resisted the temptation, and now, at the end of his ministry here on earth, Jesus tells his disciples that he has the very thing that Satan had promised him. He has all authority, both in heaven and on earth.

The second statement that bookends the commission is found in verse 20. It's a promise that as the disciples carry out the commission they can always be assured of Christ's presence. He will be with them right to the end of the age. We don't carry out the commission on our own. The book of Acts clearly shows that this was no small task. The disciples faced tremendous opposition. They were going to need this promise. They needed to know that they were not alone.

So the commission is bookended between a statement of ultimate authority and a promise of continual presence. Now let's look at the commission itself.

The commission contains four actions that must happen if it is to be faithfully carried out. First, those who are commissioned must go. Then they must make disciples. Third, they must baptize. Finally, they must teach.

We are not left to wonder which of these four is the main thrust of the passage. Only one of the verbs used is actually a command. It's the main verb from which the other verbs draw their significance. The primary focus is the command to *"make disciples."* The other three verbs—*go, baptizing,* and *teaching*—describe how this should be done.

Too often we have made the word *go* the main focus of these verses. Whether we translate it as a command, as it is in most translations (simply "go") or as a participle as some commentators would suggest ("while going" or "when you go"), it's not the primary verb in the sentence. In order to fulfill the Great Commission, we need to go. We will never succeed by staying within the safe confines of our churches. As

Rebecca Manley Pippert suggests in her best-selling book of a few years ago, we need to get "out of the saltshaker and into the world."[57] I have always loved that book title because of the vivid picture it suggests. Salt does no one any good when it's in the saltshaker. To be effective, it has to be shaken out of its safe environment.

As essential as going is, though, it's not the primary focus of the Great Commission. Over the years countless people have preached powerful sermons on the need for people to go. In response, Christians have committed themselves to missionary service in every corner of the globe. We can rejoice in the impact that such sermons have had, but we do need to question the exegesis behind the sermons. When the focus is on going instead of on making disciples, we miss the impact of what Jesus is telling us to do.

The second element in fulfilling the commission is baptism. It is beyond the scope of this book to give a detailed theological explanation of the significance of baptism. Theologians and church leaders have argued over the significance of baptism, the method by which it is practiced, and at what stage in a person's life it should take place. While these questions are important and every church should have an answer to them, they aren't relevant to our study here.

I want to focus on one truth about baptism. Baptism is the initiation into the church. Throughout the book of Acts baptism always accompanied conversion. It was the outward sign of the inward change that was taking place. When the people on the Day of Pentecost asked Peter what they needed to do to be saved, he responded by saying that they needed to repent and be baptized (Acts 2:37–38). Baptism is the outward sign of an inward reality. We don't become part of the Body of Christ by being baptized, but baptism is the symbol of the change that has taken place and our incorporation into the church universal because of that change.

The process of making disciples is to happen within the context of the local church. It is only within the church that the lifelong disciplining process can happen. God is in the business of forming oak trees, not flowers that bloom for a summer and then are gone. Growing into maturity in our faith is a lifelong process, and it's the church that's able to invest in people from birth to death. There have been para-church organizations that have specialized in some aspect of discipleship, but they're not equipped to commit for the long term. They might be able to help the churches by providing teaching in specific areas, but the church is called to do the job.

The final aspect of the discipleship process is teaching. Growth requires content. We are to teach all that Jesus commanded. This would suggest that one of the most important tasks of church leadership is to determine the content of the teaching in their church. Are they teaching all that Jesus commanded? Are there specific things that need to be taught if the process of making disciples is going to be successful? How much teaching is required for this process to be successful?

Having looked briefly at what is involved in making disciples, let's look at the main thrust of the commission, the actual command that Jesus gave to his followers. If we are going to carry out the commission, it's essential that we understand exactly what we are to do.

We Are to Make Disciples

Whatever else our vision for the church might include and however we might word our vision statement, it must include this single fact. We are called to make disciples. Dallas Willard makes this point very well:

> The word "disciple" occurs 269 times in the New Testament. "Christian" is found three times and was first introduced to refer precisely to disciples of Jesus—in a situation where it was no longer possible to regard them as a sect of the Jews (Acts 11:26). The New Testament is a book about disciples, by disciples and for disciples of Jesus Christ.[58]

There are two very simple and yet profound questions that we must answer if we are to obey this command:

1. What is a disciple?
2. What do we have to do to make one?

In answering the first question, there are two common ways of understanding this command, both of which are wrong. The first is that this command is a call to missions. As I have already alluded to, this understanding comes out of putting too much emphasis on the first participle rather than on the main command. The challenge here is not to do cross-cultural missions. The challenge is not to "go" to a different part of the world or to a different culture in our own country. The challenge is to "make disciples," and that happens as we go.

When we use these verses as a challenge to "go" we are advocating a wrong concept of mission. Mission is not what we do someplace else. It is what the church is called to do in every aspect of church life. Mission is what we do within our own neighbourhoods. Mission is what we do as we carry out the task of making disciples in whatever geographical location we find ourselves. We are called to the task of making disciples. God will decide the geographical and cultural setting in which we carry out the task.

The primary emphasis of this passage is not a call to missions. It is also not a call just to evangelism. If Jesus was simply calling his followers to be involved in sharing their faith, he could have used a number of other words here. He didn't use those words. He used the verb form of the word that we translate as "disciple." This is a very important distinction to make.

When we interpret the commission here to mean simply evangelism, we limit its meaning in a way that the passage does not allow. Too often we think of evangelism as our witness to those who are not Christians. It is limited to a very narrow part of a person's life, the part that occurs before she takes the step of faith that results in her becoming a Christian.

Making disciples has a far broader connotation. Rather than being limited to just one part of a person's life, it applies to the entirety of our lives. The job of becoming a disciple doesn't end when we make a decision to follow Christ. It continues until we are with Jesus Christ in glory. We are always on that growth path that is part of the transformation that God is working in our lives. As churches we need to see the commission in these terms. We need to understand the full scope of the task that we have been given.

So the Great Commission is not a call to missions, and it is not a call solely to evangelism. It may include both of these but is much more than either of them.

Let's return to the first question: *What is a disciple?* There have been many definitions offered for what constitutes a disciple. I want to look at three and from these three form a definition of what it means to make disciples.

Dietrich Bonhoeffer defined it in terms of adherence to Jesus Christ.[59] In that adherence to Christ, there must be a willingness to pay a price.

> As we embark upon discipleship we surrender ourselves to Christ in union with his death—we give over our lives to death. Thus it begins; the cross is not the terrible end to an otherwise God-fearing and happy life, but it meets us at the beginning of our communion with Christ. When Christ calls a man, he bids him come and die.[60]

Greg Ogden stresses the aspect of ongoing growth until we reach maturity in Christ:

> Discipline is an intentional relationship in which we walk alongside other disciples in order to encourage, equip and challenge one another in love to grow toward maturity in Christ. This includes equipping the disciple to teach others as well.[61]

Jonathan Wilson reminds us that the Great Commission is to be carried out in the context of community:

> I begin with the importance of community not because it is the first or most important part of the commission that Jesus gave, though both may be argued. Rather, I begin with community because this aspect is the most neglected and least recognized. When Jesus commissions his disciples, he commissions them as a whole, not as individuals. Certainly we see Peter, Paul and

other individuals preaching, but even that act of witness is an act of the whole church through their common life.[62]

Let's look at each of these three factors and then bring them together into a definition.

Adherence to Christ

Discipleship is always defined by a commitment to a person, and for the Christian that person must be Jesus Christ. Our adherence is not to a doctrinal system or a church or a group of people. It is to the One who is central to the whole Christian faith.

The process of discipleship is learning what it means to belong to Jesus Christ. It is learning to live our lives not according to our own wishes any longer but as people who belong to Jesus. It is allowing our lives to be shaped and moulded by the One to whom we have surrendered them. Therein lies the challenge of discipleship.

Growth into Maturity

Being confident of this, that he who began a good work in you will carry it on to completion until the day of Christ Jesus. (Philippians 1:6)

The older I become, the more I love that verse. When I was young I lived with the illusion that the day would come when I would have reached maturity and I wouldn't have to worry any longer about the battle with sin and failure in my life. I could come to love the doctrine of sinless perfection if I could just convince myself that it is biblical. Unfortunately, I have never been able to do that. I could love the thought that the day could come during my life here on earth when I would no longer have to battle against sin, but I know that I will never see that day this side of heaven. Actually, a strange thing has happened as I've grown older. Rather than reach a point at which I no longer sin, I have become more and more conscious of the extent of sin in my life. I feel that I'm farther away from perfection now than I was when I was twenty. I've come to realize that in this life the battle is never going to be over. But—and it's a huge "but"—

the promise is there that the day is coming when Jesus will have done his work in me and the battle will be over. I will be perfect, not because I have somehow in my own strength achieved perfection, but because Jesus Christ will have completed his work. That will be an amazing day.

Here on earth our lives are a slow growth into maturity. Jesus Christ is gradually making us into the people he wants us to be. I take great encouragement in that fact. I am not at all what I should be, but by the grace of God I am more than I was yesterday or last year or ten years ago. Disciple-making involves helping people grow into oak trees, and that takes time.

Partnership in Each Other's Lives

I have a confession to make. I'm a long-term reader of Louis L'Amour. Now for those who have never heard of Mr. L'Amour, he was the most popular writer of Western fiction in the history of publishing. His books sold millions of copies. Incorporated into his books were little pieces of his personal philosophy. You would read these tidbits of wisdom in almost every book that he wrote. One of the things that he always had someone in his book say was that the truly strong person is the person who stands alone. To the extent that he relied on another person, to that extent he weakened himself.

That might be good frontier wisdom, but it's terrible theology. God put us in a church because he knew that, rather than strength coming from self-reliance, true strength comes only when we allow other people into our lives. One of Paul's most popular pictures for the church was that of a body, because all of the members in a body need the other members to survive.

Almost every discipleship program that I know is designed to occur either as an individual study or with just a couple of other people. I believe that there is a place for these kinds of studies. They can augment the discipleship process and do so very effectively, but they should never stand alone. Making disciples is something that is designed to take place in the context of the whole church.

One of the most misunderstood words in the New Testament is *fellowship*. Too often it is understood only in terms of social events in our churches, giving rise to the expression "fun, food and fellowship." It has a much deeper meaning, one that is important to understand in the context of our study of the process of making disciples. John Stott describes three aspects of true biblical fellowship:

> Let me now summarize the threefold aspects which koinonia wears in the New Testament. It speaks of our common inheritance (what we share in together), of our co-operative service (what we share out together), and of our reciprocal responsibility (what we share with one another). In the first we are receiving together, in the second we are giving together, while in the third there is a mutual give and take.[63]

I like to think of fellowship as an investment. As Christians we invest ourselves (our material resources, time, talents, spiritual gifts, counsel, caring, and so on) into the lives of our fellow believers. In turn they are to invest themselves into our lives. In this mutual giving of ourselves to each other, growth occurs, and we experience what it means to grow in our walk with God. It's in the context of mutual investment in each other that true fellowship occurs, and it's in this context of true fellowship that the church carries out its role as disciple-makers.

So these three elements are essential if we are going to fulfill the Great Commission and make disciples. A disciple is someone who is living with a strong relationship to Jesus Christ. He is someone who is experiencing a gradual transformation of his life over time. Finally, he is someone who is living out that relationship with Christ and experiencing that transformation in the context of a local church.

Let's now bring these three concepts together into a definition:

> A disciple is someone who is in a personal relationship with Jesus Christ, is growing into maturity within that relationship, and is living out that relationship in the context of the local church community.

This brings us to the second question: *What does the church need to do to make those kinds of disciples?*

This question is seldom asked by church leaders. If we are going to carry out the commission that Jesus Christ has given to us, it's the most important question that we can ask, and yet most churches never ask it. What do we need to do to be successful in the task of making disciples?

Again, I'm not going to provide an easy three-step program that will enable you to become disciple-makers. That's a question that every church needs to wrestle with in the context of their unique situation. Each church needs to answer this question in the context of its own distinctive beliefs and practices. Your church needs to have the goal clearly in mind. Once you have defined what a disciple is, then you need to determine what you need to do to produce those kinds of people.

TEN

Building a Vision

In this chapter we come to the final step in the process of developing a vision for what God wants your church to be and do. You have run a reality check to determine what really is the truth about your church. Any vision must be developed out of that reality. There must be an acceptance that a program developed in a different church located in a different geographical setting with a different culture is not going to work for your church. There must be an acceptance of who God has made you to be and of the location in which God has placed you to work. There must be an understanding of your strengths and weaknesses, of your mix of giftedness and of your unique makeup. Only when you have defined reality for your situation are you ready to develop a vision for what might be.

You have recognized the fact that leadership in any church is important. You are committed to developing a leadership team that is built around spiritual vitality, character, giftedness, growth, servanthood, and courage. You, as a leadership team, are committed to accountability and ongoing growth. You have given your leadership team freedom to lead. You are committed to following that kind of leadership.

You have discovered your own uniqueness as a church with a commitment to build around that uniqueness. While you are anxious to discover the principles that other churches are employing, you understand that outside programs are not going to provide you with the vision that you need. As part of the discovery process you have embraced the value of the small church. You believe that small churches can have an impact in their own right. Relationships are everything in a small church, and you are committed to developing the kind of relationships that can have an impact on people within and outside of your church family.

You are prepared to think through some theological truths that may be hindering your church. You are excited to be part of God's mission here on earth, realizing that your purpose for existence rests in coming alongside God in the fulfillment of that mission. You realize that at the heart of everything that Jesus did was his belief that the Kingdom of God had become a reality here on earth in his person and work. You are part of that Kingdom, and your challenge is to see that Kingdom lived out through the lives of individual members and your corporate life as a church. You have broadened your understanding of conversion, realizing that evangelism is much more than just getting people to pray a prayer.

The challenge is to create a setting in which people can understand the content of what they are believing, where people can experience the kind of turning that is essential to conversion, and where people can live out the wonder of transformed lives as they become part of God's family, with all that that entails.

Finally, you have embraced the fact that the Great Commission is a call to make disciples. It is a call for the church to bring people from that first moment of interest in the gospel to a point at which they are fully mature, fully functioning followers of Jesus Christ. The content of this chapter is what is involved in this disciple-making process.

One of the great experiences of my life occurred in 1978 when I participated in the Billy Graham crusade that was held in the old Maple Leaf Gardens and CNE Stadium in Toronto. I had the privilege of serving as one of the counsellors to the counsellors. When people came forward, I was available if one of the counsellors needed help. I was one of the first people on the infield in front of the stage area when the invitation was given, which meant that I had a great location from which to watch people coming forward.

I will always remember the final service, on Sunday afternoon, at which thousands of people came forward to commit their lives to Jesus Christ. It was an amazing sight. Every aisle in the stadium was packed with people as seekers and counsellors made their way down the stairs and onto the infield. The sight of so many people responding to the invitation is indelibly imprinted in my memory.

There's something marvelous when a person responds to the gospel of Jesus Christ, in whatever setting that response might take place. For a Christian there's the excitement of knowing that the person is moving from a life without Christ into a brand new relationship with the living God.

As exciting as this is, though, it's *not* what we as a church have been called to do. We have not been called to get people to make decisions for Christ. That statement may sound like heresy to some, but it's true. On the basis of the Great Commission, our task is not to get people to make decisions.

I expect that there are some who are about to write me off at this point, but please, hear me through. That *is* part of what we are called to do, but only part. When someone puts his faith in Christ, the job is only partially done. We are called not to get decisions but to make disciples, and that job involves much, much more. It involves a longer investment of time and energy into someone's life than simply getting them to pray a prayer so that we can mark it up as another decision. The church is called to make a long-term investment in people that extends from the moment when they first express an interest in the gospel to the time when God calls them home to be with him in heaven. Becoming a fully mature, fully functioning follower of Jesus Christ is a lifelong process, and for that reason the church's commitment to people must be a lifelong commitment.

With this in mind, there are several questions that churches must ask themselves if they are going to be faithful to the task to which they have been called. First, is the Great Commission still the mandate for the church in the twenty-first century? Do the final words of Jesus to the church still define what the church is to be doing? Is the church still called to make disciples in our postmodern world, or do we need to look somewhere else for our mandate?

If your answer is that the Great Commission is no longer relevant, then you should stop reading right now, because nothing in the remainder of this chapter will matter. But if your answer is that Christ's commission never changes and we are still called to obey it, I encourage you to read on.

Second, if we are still called to make disciples, what do we need to do for that to happen? I'll repeat that question, because I believe it's the single most important question that a church can ask, and yet very few churches ever ask it.

If we are called to make disciples, what do we need to do for that to happen?

In order to answer, we need to develop a whole new way of viewing evangelism. Rather than seeing it as an attempt to get people to make a decision for Christ, we need to see it as a process by which we get people to make a whole series of decisions, including a decision to put their faith in Christ but also involving a series of steps designed to produce ongoing growth in their lives as disciples of Jesus Christ. We need to see becoming a Christian as just one step in the process of becoming a disciple—an absolutely crucial step, but nevertheless one step in a series of decisions. The church has a responsibility to lead people through all of the steps necessary, including that step of initial faith.

This is where the previous question becomes so important. What are the steps that a person needs to go through in order to become a mature follower of Jesus? What are the essential elements of discipleship? What things are critical for a person to grow in his faith until he becomes a mature believer? These are the questions that every church should be asking. Everything a church does should be designed to be part of bringing people to full discipleship.

I'm going to suggest a number of elements that are important, but the list is not meant to be definitive. Every church needs to develop its own list. Every church needs to work through a whole range of issues, asking itself how important each element is in the process of making disciples. When a church has developed its own list of eight or ten elements, it is ready to immerse itself in the wonderful world of disciple-making.

Initial Interest

Over the years I have been involved in a number of evangelistic efforts in which the purpose was to create opportunities to share the gospel with total strangers. I have gone door to door with surveys. I have set up a booth at a fall fair at which people could take surveys. I have handed out tracts on the street. I have preached at an outdoor church service in a mall parking lot with the hope that strangers would listen. None of those attempts were particularly successful.

The problem was that we were pushing people to make a decision before they had even expressed an interest. This kind of evangelism is a little like going to someone's door and introducing her to a total stranger and suggesting that she should marry him. We laugh at the thought and have no doubt as to what she would say, and yet that is what we often do when we share our faith. We come to someone who doesn't even know who Jesus is and ask her to make the most radical commitment that anyone can ever make, without giving her any opportunity to get to know this One to whom we are asking her to commit her life.

This is why relationships are so important in evangelism. The question that every church should be asking is not how do we do evangelism with strangers but how do we encourage our members to build relationships with friends and neighbours so that they can slowly introduce the subject of Christianity into that relationship.

The initial decision that every person needs to make is whether she will put herself into a setting in which she has contact with Christians. She needs to decide whether she will even open her life to the possibility of hearing about Jesus Christ. Too often people rush to a presentation of the gospel when the seeker is still deciding whether she even wants to associate with Christian people.

For the most part, Christians are the most generous, caring, giving people that you will ever meet. I know that Christians have taken a lot of criticism over the years for being dogmatic in their beliefs, and I also know that some of it is justified. But my experience has been that when there is a need, Christian people respond in an incredibly generous way. There is something very powerful in exposing unchurched people to the love and concern that is in most of our churches. I could fill a book with examples of individual Christians who have responded to the needs of people around them.

Every church needs to have doors by which people can safely enter into church life so that they are exposed to the love and care that is there. These doors can be anything—social events, community activities, Bible studies, seminars—that provide people with an opportunity to meet church people. These need to be seen as simply doors by which people enter. They are the first steps in the person's journey.

The emphasis needs to be on building relationships rather than on preaching the gospel. Sometimes we think that we aren't doing evangelism unless there is a full gospel presentation at every event. There needs to be activities to which people can come without feeling pressured in any way, and that might mean that there is no pressure on them to respond to the gospel on their first visit.

What doors are there in your church for people to enter so that they meet your church members?

Understanding Content

Earlier in the book I stated that most churches don't have a setting in which the content of the gospel is explained. If a person is going to take a step of faith, there must be content to that faith. If there is going to be content to a person's faith, that content must be shared and explained so that the person understands what she is responding to.

We live in a culture in which fewer and fewer people have been exposed to the content of the Bible. There was a time when even the person who didn't go to church had a basic understanding of the gospel. Quite possibly he had gone to Sunday school as a child and knew the basic stories of the Bible. That is no longer the case. Many of the people with whom we have contact have never been inside of a church in their lives except to attend a wedding or a funeral. More and more funerals are being held in funeral homes and weddings in a whole variety of settings, which means that they might not even have been in a church for those occasions. There are more and more people who do not know even the basics of the Christian faith.

Once people have made the decision to be around Christian people, there needs to be a setting in which they can hear the content of the gospel. They need to understand who Jesus is. They need to be made aware of the sinfulness of the human race and of their own sin. They need to understand the importance of Christ's death on the cross. They need to understand that salvation is by faith alone and involves a personal commitment to Jesus Christ.

My point here is not to give an outline of the gospel but to suggest that within every church's structure there needs to be a place in which the basic content of the gospel can be taught. This could be in a special class or a home Bible study or any number of other settings, but it needs to be there. People need to be invited to make a decision to hear the gospel message so that they can make the next decision, to respond to it.

A Response to the Gospel

Too often this is where we want to begin in our evangelism. We want to pressure people into making a decision to become a Christian before they are ready. People need to understand what it is that they are being challenged to accept. They need to understand the content of the gospel. We need to have those first two steps in place as part of our outreach before we ask people to respond to the invitation to become a Christian. So many of the evangelistic efforts in which I have played a part over the years have failed to do that.

When my wife and I were living in Barranquilla, Colombia, as part of a church planting team, we spent a lot of time going door-to-door selling Bibles and books. This was the first step in a process that included home Bible studies and friendship evangelism. While we were doing this we met a group of North Americans who were also doing evangelism, as part of a summer missions project. They were going door to door playing a taped short gospel message for anyone who would listen. At the end of the message the tape would invite the person to pray the sinner's prayer along with the person on the tape. The visitors would then leave them with a booklet and move on to the next house.

When we met them, they were all excited because they had been doing this for several weeks and hundreds of people had prayed the prayer and supposedly become Christians. I'm sure that they went home at the end of the summer telling everyone who would listen that they had been part of one of the most successful evangelism campaigns ever.

What they didn't understand was that in that culture, no one would ever have said no to them. Refusing to pray the prayer would have been a much more serious violation of what was considered acceptable manners than praying the prayer and not meaning anything they said. The vast majority of the people would have prayed the prayer just to be polite, with no understanding of what they were doing. This is what happens when our whole focus is on getting people to pray a prayer without any concern about whether they understand the content of the gospel.

The other danger is that we can focus entirely on building relationships and never get around to challenging people to make a decision. I believe strongly in the need to see evangelism as a process in which we build relationships and teach people the content of what they need to believe. There is, however, a very real need to challenge people to take a step of faith and become a Christian.

Sharing our faith is a process in which we respect people's need for time as they think through the implications of the gospel on their lives. Becoming a Christian is a faith decision that happens in a moment of time. People need to be challenged to make that faith decision.

I had both of these parts of the process brought home to me several years ago when I was teaching an evangelistic Bible study to a young couple who had started to attend our church. We had been working through John Stott's book *Basic Christianity* and had come to the point at which Stott challenges people to make a decision. I asked them if they were ready to take that step. The husband said, "No." He needed more time to think it all through. I said that was fine, but I was going to ask him again the next week.

When I arrived the next week, before we even got into the study, he said he had thought it through and was ready to become a Christian. If I had pressured him the first week, it's very unlikely that he would have responded the second week. He needed time, but he also needed to be challenged. I could have just moved on to other things when he said "No," but I knew how important this was. He needed to know that I was going to give him all the time he needed but I was also going to come back to his need to make a decision.

The Ordinances
Churches need to think through the place that baptism and the Lord's Supper have in the spiritual growth of Christians. In the church tradition I grew up in, both were considered to be symbolic acts that pointed to a deeper spiritual truth. Baptism pointed to the transformation that had taken place in the believer's life when he became a Christian. When he was immersed in the water, it symbolized his death to the old life, and when he was brought up out of the water, it symbolized the new life that he had in Christ. Basically, baptism was a symbolic act that one did in obedience to Christ's command.

In the Lord's Supper the bread symbolized the broken body of Christ and the cup symbolized the shed blood of Christ. The service was a remembrance service, which once again was carried out in obedience to the command of Christ. While it was important to partake in the service, there was no real spiritual benefit derived from that participation.

There has been a great deal of theological debate around all of the details of these two ordinances. There has been debate around how people should be baptized, when in our lives it should take place, and the impact of baptism on our relationship with God and the church. There have been an equal number of debates around the Lord's Supper: how often should it be held, the spiritual significance of the bread and the wine, and the importance of the act on our spiritual walk. These are issues that every church needs to work through for itself. I want to challenge each church on only one point. What place does the celebration of these ordinances have on a person becoming a fully mature disciple of Jesus Christ? If they are an important part, how does the church encourage people to make a decision to participate in them?

Christian Fellowship
The story is told of a member of a small church in Scotland who for an unknown reason stopped attending the Sunday morning service. After a period of time in which he didn't show up for even one service, the

pastor paid him a visit. The member welcomed the pastor and invited him to have a seat near the fireplace.

After sitting in silence for a period of time, the pastor stood up, moved to the fireplace, and removed a single coal from the fire. He set the coal by itself on the hearth and returned to his seat. The two men watched that coal as it slowly lost its heat. After a long period of silence the pastor got up and left. The man was in the service the next Sunday.

God did not design the church as an optional activity. He knew that all of us need the input of other believers if we are going to keep the fire burning within us. When things are going well, we need to share our joy with other people. When things are tough, we need the strength that other people bring. We all need people with whom we can share the Christian walk.

What place does Christian fellowship play in a person's growth into discipleship?

I have come to realize that going to church is largely a matter of habit. I was raised in a setting in which attendance at church every Sunday was just a part of life. In fact, I still feel guilty whenever I am not in church, even when I have a totally legitimate reason for not being there. It is hard to shake those feelings of guilt from my childhood. Whatever I might do on a Saturday evening, I know that I am going to get up the next day and go to church.

If a person did not grow up going to church, he may not think that way. He will need to be challenged to make a decision to incorporate regular attendance as a part of his life. This is especially true if his children are in hockey or one of the many other activities that occur on Sunday morning.

Spiritual Disciplines

In my childhood I was taught that the Christian life was largely defined by what I *didn't* do. A Christian was someone who did not drink alcohol, smoke cigarettes, or play cards. I could go to movies and attend high school dances, but my wife was taught that those were wrong as well. When I started dating her, I gave those two things up. After all, what's the point of going to a dance if the girl you want to take can't go with you? I preferred to spend my Saturday evenings doing things that I could do with Gloria rather than attending a dance or movie without her. I was the world's worst dancer anyway, so it wasn't much of a sacrifice.

For the most part the Christian life was defined by the things that one couldn't do, but there was one thing that I was told every good Christian did do. If you were going to grow in your walk with God, you had to have a devotional time each and every day. It was incredibly important to read your Bible and pray at the start of every day. If you were really spiritual, you would read through your Bible each and every year, and there were guides that showed you what you had to read each day in order to succeed in this. There were devotional guides that you could read every morning that would also help to get your day off to the proper start.

Even though I was told that this was a very important thing for Christians to do and something that every truly spiritual person would do, I was never once asked if I was doing it or if I was struggling and needed help. It was considered an important but very private part of what it meant to be a Christian. It was not considered good Christian etiquette to ask anyone about it. Like many young people, I struggled with my devotional life, but I struggled alone.

I believe that time spent with God is very important. I believe that there is great value in consistently reading the Word of God, in spending time in prayer, and in practicing the other spiritual disciplines. But I don't think that it's a duty that every good Christian needs to do. I gave up that approach to my devotional life a long time ago. Rather, I believe that it's important because it deepens my relationship with God. I no longer worry if I miss a day. Now I enjoy the fact that when I do regularly practice the spiritual disciplines, my walk with God becomes more meaningful. I know that if I miss a day, God is there the next day, waiting for me to spend time with him. My quiet time is an enjoyable time with God rather than a duty that must be fulfilled.

How does the church ensure that people are having a meaningful devotional life? How many people in the church are even having a quiet time with God on any sort of a regular basis? How do we help people to see this as a privilege rather than an obligation? Is it a natural part of church life to talk about the blessings or struggles that people are having in their devotional lives? Building a devotional time into busy schedules is a decision that people need to make.

Christian Service

Christians are made to serve. There can be no doubt whatsoever about that. Every follower of Jesus Christ has been called to serve in some capacity. As I mentioned earlier, every Christian has been given a spiritual gift, a supernatural endowment that equips her to serve in some capacity. The concept of spiritual gifts means much more than that we have an obligation to serve. It means that God has equipped us to serve in a way that will be fulfilling and rewarding. If someone has been given the gift of teaching, it isn't just that she needs to teach as a duty. She needs to teach because that is who God has made her to be, and if she doesn't teach, she's going to miss out on the excitement of being used by God to make a difference for the Kingdom. Whatever gift a person has, she needs to exercise that gift, because her life will be the poorer if she doesn't.

Finding an avenue in which you can use your gift is an absolutely essential part of spiritual growth. The church is called on to challenge people and to help people find that avenue of service. The church needs to help people discover their spiritual gifts and then channel people into some area of service in which that gift can be used. Christians need to be challenged to make a decision to serve.

A Christian Mindset

Too often the decision to become a Christian is presented as a simple decision with few serious implications attached to it. All a person has to do is pray a prayer and he has become a Christian. In the section on conversion I have already tried to refute this approach to evangelism. Becoming a Christian is a life-changing commitment to an entirely new way of thinking and acting that should affect every part of a person's life. It is far more than just a new approach to life. It is a change that a person goes through that impacts the very core of who that person is. Words can't express the depth of transformation that takes place. The Bible describes it as a whole new creation that has been formed (2 Corinthians 5:17). How do you get more radical than that?

A new creation requires a new mindset, a new way of thinking, a new approach to everything that the person faces in life. An important part of being a disciple is to learn to think in an entirely new way. Christianity is meant to affect how we respond to our families, our fellow workers, our friends and neighbours, and everyone else who is a part of our lives. As Christians we need to develop a whole new set of ethics so that we respond differently when we are faced with issues of honesty and integrity, when we see injustice in our world, when we are confronted with poverty, when we try to make sense of politics or the arts or some other part of our culture, when we play sports or have a disagreement with our neighbour.

I know of no bigger challenge for a church than that of teaching people to think Christianly about issues. I'm not talking about a set of rules that we try to apply to whatever situation we find ourselves in. I'm talking about a mindset, a way of thinking, so that we respond as Christ would have responded in whatever situation we face. There's a temptation in our churches to teach our people content when they need to know principles. We teach them rules when they need to know how to think like Jesus. We teach them facts when they need to know God.

To be a disciple means to be a follower of Jesus Christ. The challenge of making disciples in our churches is to teach people to think and act as Christ thought and acted. Our teaching needs to affect how people live their lives outside the Sunday-morning context.

I've been part of many different small groups and Bible studies that all start out in the same way. At the first meeting the leader asks what we should study this time around. The more vocal members of the study offer suggestions, and finally everyone votes on a topic. Or the leader has a subject that he is particularly excited about, and he imposes that on the group. What would happen if all the teaching in every facet of church life was determined by what would contribute most to people becoming fully mature disciples of Jesus Christ? What would happen if the topics were chosen according to what area of Christian growth the group most needed?

A common mistake is to think that programs are an end in themselves. A church must have a Sunday school because that is what churches do. There must be a youth group because we need to keep our teenagers involved within the church. There must be Bible studies because good Christian people study the Bible. There must be social nights because Christian people need to get together for fun, food, and fellowship. There must be a Sunday service because Christians meet for worship on Sunday mornings. I'm not suggesting that any of these things shouldn't be a part of the church, but when they become ends in themselves, they are obstacles to the church accomplishing what it is supposed to accomplish. They should be means by which the church carries out its mandate to make disciples. A Sunday school's purpose is to begin the process of turning children into fully functioning disciples of Jesus Christ. The purpose of a youth group is to turn youth into fully functioning disciples of Jesus Christ. The purpose of a Bible study or small group is to help people grow into fully functioning disciples of Jesus Christ. At the heart of that process is teaching our children, our teenagers, and our adults how to think as Christians.

Summary

The church is called to make disciples. That is the commission that it has been given. That is the challenge it faces as it attempts to work with the people it serves. There is no more important question that the church can ask than What are the essential elements in someone moving from that first spark of interest in the gospel to that point at which he is a mature, fully functioning disciple of Jesus Christ?

I have suggested eight elements. These are not meant to be the definitive list but rather discussion starters. Are these eight really essential? Are there other things that need to be added to the list? Every church is unique, and as such every church needs to make its own list of essential elements for people to make that journey from first signs of interest to being fully functioning disciples of Jesus Christ.

Notice that each step involves a decision:

A person must make a decision to become involved with Christian people.

A person must make a decision to investigate the content of the gospel.

A person must make a decision to put his faith in Jesus Christ and his work on the cross.

A person must make a decision to be baptized and to participate in the Lord's Supper.

A person must make a decision to attend corporate worship.

A person must make a decision to incorporate a devotional time into her busy schedule.

A person must make a decision to become involved in some area of Christian service.

A person must make a decision to begin to think Christianly so that it affects every area of life.

The discipleship process is challenging people to make a series of decisions that will result in Christian growth. Each one will help to bring the person into deeper relationship with Jesus Christ.

The church does not exist to keep people happy. The church does not exist to maintain the status quo. The church does not exist to share the gospel so that people make decisions. The church does not even exist for numerical growth.

The vision for every church needs to come out of the commission that Jesus Christ gave to his followers. The church exists to make disciples, people who are in relationship with Jesus Christ, so that they can grow over time in the context of the local church.

The challenge for the church is to determine what it is that produces mature disciples of Jesus Christ and then to challenge people to make the decisions that will incorporate those things into their lives.

ELEVEN

The Place of Prayer

Over the past ten years, I have had the opportunity to visit fourteen different countries around the world. I have been to the Netherlands, Austria, Greece, Turkey, Kenya, Uganda, Rwanda, Honduras, Costa Rica, Guatemala, Ecuador, Colombia, Bolivia, and the United States. Almost all of my trips have been for business, leaving me little time to see the tourist sites in these countries. What I *have* been able to do, however, is spend a lot of time with people who live there. I've met some remarkable people. Through those people, I have been able to see the church at work and to gain a firsthand understanding of what God is doing in these countries.

A few years ago I visited the country of Honduras. Shortly after my arrival I was asked if I would attend the prayer meeting that the people with whom I was visiting attended every weekday morning at five. I was just coming to the end of one of the busiest periods of my life and was tired, so I said I would go with them if I was awake, but I wasn't going to wake up especially to be there.

Have you ever wondered if God has a sense of humour? I am here to tell you that he has. In the yard right next door to the guesthouse was a rooster with a terrible sense of timing. Every morning at four o'clock that rooster crowed and I woke up. I only missed one prayer meeting the whole time that I was there.

As much as I might joke about that rooster, I was glad that he was there. Through that early morning prayer meeting and the people in Honduras, I was introduced to a level of prayer that I had never experienced before. The people didn't just have prayer meetings like we do. Their lives were shaped by prayer. Prayer was their reflex response to every situation they faced. The early morning prayer meeting was just the beginning of what was normal life for them throughout the day. They believed in prayer in a way that I have not seen here in Canada. I wish that I could have packed whatever they had in my suitcase and brought it back with me so that I could let it loose in churches here.

In most of our churches here in Canada, prayer plays a very small part in what we do. When I was a child, Wednesday night was prayer meeting night in our church. The meeting was not well attended. The study for the most part was boring. The prayer time lacked power. I don't think that I ever attended a prayer meeting at which I felt like people were really enjoying themselves. Like the Sunday evening service, the prayer meeting was eventually abandoned, and that was a good thing. In many churches the mid-week prayer meeting has been replaced by small groups, and that has been a good thing. Especially in large churches, small groups are needed.

The problem is that in most churches that time of corporate prayer has been lost. The ineffectual, boring mid-week prayer meeting was canceled, but there was no other setting for corporate prayer instituted to take its place. As a result, there is very limited opportunity in our churches for the whole church family to come together in order to pray. This loss may be at least partially responsible for the lack of power in so many of our churches.

In this book I have outlined five steps that churches need to take to effectively carry out the commission given by Jesus Christ himself. Each one of those steps needs to be supported by the corporate and individual prayers of the church members. The church needs to establish a regular setting in which people can pray for the leadership and the church as a whole as it works through the steps outlined. That setting will be unique to each church, but it needs to be there.

I have left this chapter until last because I want it to be the last thing you read, but it's the first thing that needs to be done. Prayer isn't an add-on that can be done if people have time. It's the very heart and soul of the process of discovering your church's vision and then carrying it out.

I want to leave you with an important warning. It comes from Arnold Cook:

> Prayer is the Christian's vital breath and native air. We all promote it verbally. Every new initiative is launched with the reminder: "We must bathe this ministry in prayer." But our talk too often fails to match our walk.[64]

CONCLUSION

One of the most serious problems in any church is a lack of self-esteem on the part of the people who attend. David Ray points out the damage that this can cause:

> The dominating and most debilitating problem in a high percentage of small churches is low self-esteem, resulting in low morale. Comments like "We're just a little church," "I'm just a small church pastor," "We only have thirty in worship and twenty in Sunday school," and "We don't do as much as the big church on the corner," are common and difficult to eradicate as dandelions. Low self-esteem is a cancer that kills small churches. It reduces the amount of available money, results in poor building upkeep, repels new members, discourages leaders, erodes organizational effectiveness, changes communication from positive to negative, causes church fights, undermines planning and limits relationships with those outside. In short, it undermines the ministry and mission of the church.[65]

Low self-esteem is overcome when the small church understands its own unique value. The small-church needs to understand that it is different but not of lesser value. It needs to understand its unique qualities that characterize it and give it the potential to be a force for good in the world. The small church needs to have a correct biblical understanding of its worth.

CONCLUSION

A church needs to have a vision built around the Great Commission, because that commission has been given to the church by Jesus Christ himself. It is his vision for his church. There really is no other reason to take the steps that I have outlined in this book. There are, however, benefits that come from building your vision around this challenge of making disciples. These benefits are not the reason for making this your vision, but they should be enjoyed when you do.

One of those benefits is many opportunities for a church to rejoice as its members grow into mature, fully functioning disciples of Jesus Christ. Churches do not celebrate nearly enough. In many of our churches, joy isn't forbidden but is highly frowned upon. When I was a teenager, I was taking part in a communion service in which the pastor asked a relatively new Christian to give thanks for one of the emblems. I have never forgotten his prayer. He began it with these words: "Lord, please put a smile on people's faces. They all look like they just lost their best friend." In that particular setting at that particular time, it was a very appropriate prayer to pray.

Once you have determined the elements that your church believes are essential to the process of making disciples, why not celebrate the victories in each of those areas? Celebrate the contacts that people are making with non-Christian friends and neighbours. Celebrate when church members have the opportunity to share the gospel with someone. Celebrate every person who makes a commitment of faith and becomes a Christian. Celebrate the person who has struggled with his devotional life and has attained some level of consistency. Celebrate the new Christian who has discovered her spiritual gift and is going to be teaching Sunday school. Celebrate those young people who go on mission trips or to Bible college, because that's going to be an important part of that young person's growth. Celebrate every person who decides that he is going to join the church and become a regular part of what happens within the church family. Celebrate every victory that someone has over an addictive habit in her life.

Celebrate! Celebrate! Celebrate! Celebrate! Celebrate! Celebrate!

People want to participate in what is rewarded, so reward every step that a person takes in the discipleship process. You will find if you do that people will become excited about your church, and out of that excitement will come a high level of self-esteem.

The challenge given to the church by Christ himself is to grow his church, not by filling more and more pews in the sanctuary but by developing people into fully functioning disciples of Jesus Christ. The healthy church is not the one with the most people attending on a Sunday morning but rather the one with the highest percentage of members on the road to becoming disciples.

May God bless you as you take up the challenge of making disciples so that his church becomes all that he intends it to be.

ABOUT THE AUTHOR

Dr. Ron Johnston has more than forty years of ministry experience in Canada and internationally. He has more than twenty years of pastoral experience, serving in both rural and urban settings, and has planted churches in Canada and in Colombia, South America. For the past ten years he has served with International Teams Canada, the last two as the director of international programs, overseeing ministries in Europe, Africa, Latin America and Asia. Dr. Johnston has BTh and MDiv degrees from Tyndale University College and Seminary and a DMin degree from Acadia University. During his studies at Acadia he wrote his thesis on the subject of evangelism in the small church. He has been married to Gloria for more than forty years and has three children and seven grandchildren. He has a deep love for small churches, having spent his entire life in some form of small-church ministry.

The author may be contacted at:

Small Church Connections
23 Kingfisher Drive
Elmira, ON, Canada
N3B 3K4
519-500-6580
johnston.ron@gmail.com

BIBLIOGRAPHY

Abraham, William J. *The Logic of Evangelism.* Grand Rapids: William B. Eerdmans Publishing Company, 1989.

Barna, George. *The Power of Vision: How You Can Capture and Apply God's Vision for Your Ministry.* Ventura, CA: Regal Books, 1992.

Bonhoeffer, Dietrich. *The Cost of Discipleship.* New York: Macmillan Publishing Co., 1949, 1963.

Burt, Steve. *Activating Leadership in the Small Church: Clergy and Laity Working Together.* Valley Forge, PA: Judson Press, 1988.

Clapp, Rodney. *A Peculiar People: The Church as Culture in a Post-Christian Society.* Downers Grove, IL: InterVarsity Press, 1996.

Cloud, Henry. *Integrity: The Courage to Meet the Demands of Reality.* New York: Collins, 2006.

_____. *9 Things You Simply Must Do.* Nashville: Integrity Publishers, 2004.

Cloud, Henry, and John Townsend. *Boundaries in Marriage.* Grand Rapids: Zondervan, 1999.

Collins, Jim. *Good To Great: Why Some Companies Make The Leap… and Others Don't.* New York: Collins, 2001.

Cook, Arnold L. *Historical Drift.* Camp Hill, PA: Christian Publications, 2000.

BIBLIOGRAPHY

Daman, Glenn. *Shepherding the Small Church.* Grand Rapids: Kregel Publications, 2002.

Dudley, Carl S. *Making The Small Church Effective.* Nashville: Abingdon Press, 1978.

―――――. *Effective Small Churches in the Twenty-first Century.* Nashville: Abingdon Press, 2003.

Fee, Gordon D. *Philippians.* Downers Grove, IL: InterVarsity Press, 1999.

Foster, Richard J. *Celebration of Discipline.* New York: Harper & Row, 1978.

Hansen, David. *Renewing Your Church Through Vision and Planning.* Edited by Marshall Shelley. Minneapolis: Bethany House Publishers, 1997.

Helm, Paul. *The Beginnings: Word & Spirit in Conversion.* Edinburgh: The Banner of Trust, 1986.

Hybels, Bill. *Ax.i.om: Powerful Leadership Proverbs.* Grand Rapids: Zondervan, 2008.

Jones, E. Stanley. *The Reconstruction of the Church—on what pattern?* Nashville: Abingdon Press, 1979.

Kaiser, Walter C., Jr. *Mission in the Old Testament: Israel as a Light to the Nation.* Grand Rapids: Baker Books, 2000.

Ladd, George Eldon. *The Presence of the Future.* Grand Rapids: William B. Eerdmans Publishing Company, 1974.

Malphurs, Aubrey. *Being Leaders: The Nature of Authentic Christian Leadership.* Grand Rapids: Baker Books, 2003.

Ogden, Greg. *Discipleship Essentials: A Guide to Building Your Life in Christ.* Downers Grove, IL: IVP Connect, 1998.

Outreach Canada. "Church Size, Attendance and Membership." Available from http://en.outreach.ca/ServingYou/tabid/2237/Articled/916/Size-Attendance-and-Membership.aspx.

Peace, Richard V. *Conversion in the New Testament: Paul and the Twelve.* Grand Rapids: William B. Eerdmans, 1999.

Maxwell, John. *Leadership Gold.* Nashville: Thomas Nelson, 2008.

Meade, Loren B. *Inside The Small Church.* Edited by Anthony G. Pappas. Alban Institute, 2002.

Pappas, Anthony G. *Entering The World of the Small Church.* Alban Institute, 2000.

Pippert, Rebecca Manley. *Out of the Saltshaker and into the World: Evangelism as a Way of Life.* Downers Grove, IL: InterVarsity Press, 1979.

Ray, David R. *The Big Small Church Book.* Cleveland: The Pilgrim Press, 1992.

Schaller, Lyle E. *Looking In The Mirror.* Nashville: Abingdon Press, 1984.

Smith, Gordon T. *Christian Conversion & Authentic Transformation.* Downers Grove, IL: InterVarsity Press, 2001.

Stedman, Ray C. *Body Life.* Glendale, CA: G/L Regal Books, 1972.

Stott, John R. W. *Basic Christianity.* 2nd ed. Downers Grove, IL: InterVarsity Press, 1971.

Wagner, C. Peter. *Leading Your Church To Growth.* Ventura, CA: Regal Books, 1984.

_____. *Your Church Can Grow: Seven Vital Signs of a Healthy Church.* Glendale, CA: G/L Regal Books, 1976.

Warren, Rick. *The Purpose Driven Church: Growth Without Compromising Your Message & Mission.* Grand Rapids: Zondervan, 1995.

Willard, Dallas. *The Great Omission: Reclaiming Jesus' Essential Teachings on Discipleship.* San Francisco: HarperSanFrancisco, 2006.

Wilson, Jonathan R. *Why Church Matters: Worship, Ministry and Mission in Practice.* Grand Rapids: Brazon Press, 2006.

Wright, Christopher J. H. *The Mission of God: Unlocking the Bible's Grand Narrative.* Downers Grove, IL: IVP Academics, 2006.

———. *The Mission of God's People: A Biblical Theology of the Church's Mission.* Grand Rapids: Zondervan, 2010.

FOOTNOTES

1. Ray C. Stedman, *Body Life* (Glendale, CA: G/L Regal Books, 1972), 2.

2. C. Peter Wagner, *Leading Your Church to Growth* (Ventura, CA: Regal Books, 1984), 21.

3. C. Peter Wagner, *Your Church Can Grow: Seven Vital Signs of a Healthy Church* (Glendale, CA: G/L Regal Books, 1976), 49.

4. Henry Cloud, *Integrity: The Courage to Meet the Demands of Reality* (New York: Collins, 2006), 106.

5. David Hansen, *Renewing Your Church Through Vision and Planning,* ed. Marshall Shelley (Minneapolis: Bethany House Publisher, 1997), 36, 37.

6. Henry Cloud and John Townsend, *Boundaries in Marriage* (Grand Rapids: Zondervan, 1999), 51.

7. Lyle E. Schaller, *Looking in the Mirror* (Nashville: Abingdon Press, 1984), 38.

8. Bill Hybels, *Ax.i.om: Powerful Leadership Proverbs* (Grand Rapids: Zondervan, 2008), 159.

9. Henry Cloud, *9 Things You Simply Must Do* (Nashville: Integrity Publishers, 2004), 233.

10. Jim Collins, *Good To Great* (New York: Collins, 2001), 77.

11. John Maxwell, *Leadership Gold* (Nashville: Thomas Nelson, 2008), 106.

12. Collins, *Good To Great,* 70.

13. Maxwell, *Leadership Gold*, 11.

14. Gordon D. Fee, *Philippians* (Downers Grove, IL: InterVarsity Press, 1999), 143, 144.

15. Richard J. Foster, *Celebration of Discipline* (New York: Harper & Row, 1978).

16. Cloud, *Integrity*, 8.

17. Cloud, *Integrity*, 8.

18. See 1 Corinthians 4:16; 11:1; Philippians 3:17; 4:9; 1 Thessalonians 1:6; 2 Thessalonians 3:7, 9.

19. Romans 12:3–8; 1 Corinthians 12–14; Ephesians 4:11–13.

20. Schaller, *Looking in the Mirror*, 14–37.

21. Arnold L. Cook, *Historical Drift* (Camp Hill, PA: Christian Publications, 2000), 67.

22. Outreach Canada, "Church Size, Attendance and Membership." Accessed 21 March 2011, http://en.outreach.ca/ServingYou/tabid/2237/Articled/916/Church-Size-Attendance-and-Membership.aspx.

23. Schaller, *Looking in the Mirror*, 15–23.

24. Steve Burt, *Activating Leadership in the Small Church: Clergy and Laity Working Together* (Valley Forge, PA: Judson Press, 1988), 38.

25. Carl S. Dudley, *Effective Small Churches in the Twenty-First Century* (Nashville: Abingdon Press, 2003), 37–50.

26. Anthony G. Pappas, *Entering the World of the Small Church* (Alban Institute, 2000), 26.

27. David R. Ray, preface to *The Big Small Church Book* (Cleveland: The Pilgrim Press, 1992), viii.

28. Burt, *Activating Leadership*, 20–26.

29. David R. Ray, *The Big Small Church Book* (Cleveland: The Pilgrim Press, 1992), 35–41.

30. Glenn Daman, *Shepherding the Small Church* (Grand Rapids: Kregel Publications, 2002), 43–51.

31. Pappas, *Entering The World*, 139.

32. Loren B. Meade, *Inside The Small Church,* ed. Anthony G. Pappas (Alban Institute, 2002), 96.

33. Carl S. Dudley, *Making The Small Church Effective* (Nashville: Abingdon Press, 1978), 72.

34. Wagner, *Leading Your Church,* 21–22.

35. E. Stanley Jones, *The Reconstruction of the Church—on What Pattern?* (Nashville: Abingdon Press, 1970), 9.

36. Interview with the author at Pinewoods Gospel Chapel, July 14, 2011.

37. Interview with the author at Elmvale Community Church, July 20, 2011.

38. Interview with the author at Bridletowne Park Church, August 4, 2011.

39. Interview with the author at The Rock Community Church, August 2, 2011.

40. Interview with the author at New Dundee Baptist Church, August 17, 2011.

41. Christopher J. H. Wright, *The Mission of God: Unlocking the Bible's Grand Narrative* (Downers Grove, IL: IVP Academics, 2006).

42. Walter C. Kaiser Jr., *Mission in the Old Testament: Israel as a Light to the Nation* (Grand Rapids: Baker Books, 2000), 13.

43. Christopher J. H. Wright, *The Mission of God's People: A Biblical Theology of the Church's Mission* (Grand Rapids: Zondervan, 2010), 68.

44. Wright, *The Mission of God's People,* 24.

45. John R. W. Stott, *Basic Christianity,* 2nd ed. (Downers Grove, IL: InterVarsity Press, 1971), 21.

46. George Eldon Ladd, *The Presence of the Future* (Grand Rapids: William B. Eerdmans, 1974), 111–112.

FOOTNOTES

47. William J. Abraham, *The Logic of Evangelism* (Grand Rapids: William B. Eerdmans, 1989), 13.

48. Rodney Clapp, *A Peculiar People: The Church as Culture in a Post-Christian Society* (Downers Grove, IL: InterVarsity Press, 1996), 167.

49. Wright, *The Mission of God*, 319.

50. Richard V. Peace, *Conversion in the New Testament: Paul and the Twelve* (Grand Rapids: William B. Eerdmans, 1999), 37.

51. Paul Helm, *The Beginnings: Word & Spirit in Conversion* (Edinburgh: The Banner of Trust, 1986), 69–70.

52. Gordon T. Smith, *Christian Conversion & Authentic Transformation* (Downers Grove, IL: InterVarsity Press, 2001), 125.

53. Peace, *Conversion in the New Testament*, 85.

54. George Barna, *The Power of Vision: How You Can Capture and Apply God's Vision for Your Ministry* (Ventura, CA: Regal Books, 1992), 16.

55. Aubrey Malphurs, *Being Leaders: The Nature of Authentic Christian Leadership* (Grand Rapids: Baker Books, 2003), 168.

56. Rick Warren, *The Purpose Driven Church: Growth Without Compromising Your Message & Mission* (Grand Rapids: Zondervan, 1995), 137.

57. Rebecca Manley Pippert, *Out of the Saltshaker and into the World: Evangelism As a Way of Life* (Downers Grove, IL: InterVarsity Press, 1979).

58. Dallas Willard, *The Great Omission: Reclaiming Jesus' Essential Teachings on Discipleship* (San Francisco: HarperSanFrancisco, 2006), 3.

59. Dietrich Bonhoeffer, *The Cost of Discipleship* (New York: Macmillan Publishing Co., Inc., 1949, 1963), 63.

60. Bonhoeffer, *The Cost of Discipleship*, 99.

61. Greg Ogden, *Discipleship Essentials: A Guide to Building Your Life in Christ* (Downers Grove, IL: IVP Connect, 1998), 17.

62. Jonathan R. Wilson, *Why Church Matters: Worship, Ministry, and Mission in Practice* (Grand Rapids: Brazon Press, 2006), 76.

63. John Stott, *One People* (London: Falcon Books, 1968), 83.

64. Cook, *Historical Drift,* 286.

65. Ray, *The Big Small Church Book,* 141–142.